THROUGH STEVIE'S EYES

THE TALE OF A BLIND DOG

By
Marina Casanelles Gili

Copyright © 2024 Marina Casanelles Gili

All rights reserved.

No part of this publication may be reproduced, distributed, or transmitted in any form or by any means, including photocopying, recording, or other electronic or mechanical methods, without the prior written permission of the publisher, except as permitted by U.S. copyright law.

The story, all names, characters, and incidents portrayed in this production have been altered to protect the privacy of the individuals involved within this narration. No identification with actual persons (living or deceased), places, buildings, and products is intended or should be inferred.

Dedication

To my sweet boy, Stevie. Thank you for showing me the true meaning of unconditional love and resilience. This story is dedicated to you, my precious companion.

I want to acknowledge Ellen Fair's support, dedication, guidance, and assistance throughout the writing process. Thank you, Ellen, for helping me bring Stevie's story to life and sharing it with everyone.

This book is a true story about a blind dog. The author made only minimal modifications to make it easier to read while staying true to the original tale.

For videos of Stevie go to YouTube:
https://www.youtube.com/channel/UC9eWdLyQGAdBw9rXSg9m8UQ

Table Of Contents

Chapter 1: As A Puppy 1

Chapter 2: Stevie's Sightlessness 16

Chapter 3: Stevie's Lifeline 28

Chapter 4: Stevie's Remarkable Abilities 52

Chapter 5: Becoming More 79

Chapter 6: Search And Rescue Training 93

Chapter 7: Getting Ready For Certification 116

Chapter 8: Certification 125

Chapter 9: Work Well Done 143

Chapter 10: Trip To Spain 157

Chapter 11: Moving To St. Croix 178

Chapter 12: Moving To Washington State 200

Chapter 1

As A Puppy

As dusk gave way to the serene glow of a clear night, the full moon hung prominently in the sky a celestial beacon that seemed to watch over the Earth. With his seasoned intuition honed through twenty years of breeding top-notch hunting dogs, Art felt a distinctive stir of anticipation in the air. On nights such as this, tranquil and almost reverent, the very rhythms of nature seemed to align.

Lucy, Art's prized English cocker spaniel, lay nestled within the rustic confines of an old barn that Art had converted into a well-equipped breeding space. The barn itself was saturated with memories and the echoes of many litters past, and tonight, it was Lucy's turn to add to the storied legacy of Art's kennels. This was her first litter, bringing a unique blend of excitement and anxious hope to Art's experienced heart.

He had prepared a spacious pen for Lucy, lined with soft blankets to provide comfort and warmth away from any drafts or disturbances. It was his custom, a personal commitment etched through years of practice, to accompany his dogs through the birthing process. For Art, the whelping was not merely a business affair but a moment of bond and kinship with his canines.

As the clock hands moved, marking the silent passage of time, the barn remained a pocket of quiet activity. Art watched over Lucy with a vigilance that was both tender and focused. In the stillness of the night, Lucy seemed to be in a deep slumber, her breaths rhythmic and unhurried, her body sprawled in the comfort of her pen. Yet, Art knew this repose was the calm before the transformative storm of life-bringing activity.

The dogs Art bred were not just animals; they were hunters, each one bearing the lineage and the promise of field excellence. Art's love for the hunt was inseparable from his love for the breed. English cocker spaniels were his companions on the crisp morning hunts, his partners in the rustling reeds on the hunt for ducks. Each dog was an exquisite testament to Art's dedication to the sport and his unwavering standard for athleticism and aptitude.

With a distant smile, he recalled the many litters born under his watchful eye, each a chapter in his life's pursuit. The barn was an archive of those joyful and sometimes agonizing experiences of life's fragility and triumph.

It was in these quiet hours, with the consistency of the moon's watch, that Art allowed himself to reflect. Breeding was not simply a profession but a calling, a continuous reach toward perfection in his canine wards. This night, as with so many before, promised the gift of new beginnings, of puppies that would grow under his careful guidance to become the next generation of exquisite hunters. Art settled into his chair, a steadfast sentinel, waiting for Lucy to stir for the first signs of labor to commence. He was ready, as he had always been, to assist in the miraculous arrival of new life a time-honored ritual that filled him with pride and a profound sense of purpose.

As the clock hands inched their way toward midnight, Art kept a watchful yet patient eye on Lucy. Nestled within the confines of the barn, the stillness was occasionally punctured by the soft rustling of straw as Lucy grew increasingly restless. Her unease was a telltale sign to Art; decades of breeding experience whispered to him that the pivotal moment of whelping was drawing near.

In response to Lucy's mounting anxiety, Art stepped closer, assuming the role he had played countless times before part midwife, part comforting presence. His voice dipped into tranquility as he spoke to his trusted companion. "Breathe, sweet Lucy. I am here, and everything will be okay," he murmured. Words were beyond Lucy's comprehension, but the soothing timbre of Art's voice was a balm, a familiar sound that eased her into a state of relative calm.

The night crept onward, and the barn's shadows played against the walls as Art waited. A few hours later, he began to notice the unmistakable signs of labor progressing Lucy's abdomen tensed rhythmically with contractions. Observing with growing attentiveness, Art prepared himself mentally for the task ahead.

It wasn't long before the first puppy entered the world. Within moments, and with practiced hands, Art greeted the newborn. Cradling the small, wet bundle in a clean towel, he carefully cleared its nose and mouth, ensuring the puppy's breath would not be hindered by the remnants of its amniotic cradle. Gently, he rubbed the towel over the tiny animal, stimulating circulation and evoking the first gasps of air into its lungs.

Now breathing and showing signs of life, the puppy was carefully placed adjacent to Lucy, who instinctively took over. With motherly diligence, she began to lick and nuzzle her offspring, her tongue cleaning and stimulating her pup. This sequence continued, a rhythm that nature herself seemed to orchestrate, and approximately every half-hour, another puppy joined the growing litter.

Art had been privy to an ultrasound image some time ago; he knew that Lucy carried eight precious lives within her. One by one, they came forth each separated by the briefest span of creation until all eight lay wriggling and mewling beside their mother. They were a picture of health, complete with all their tiny toes.

After ensuring each puppy was cared for, Art turned his attention to the remnants of birth. The placentas were carefully removed from the pen and delivered in due course with each puppy. His eyes then turned back to the scene of Lucy tenderly coaxing her pups to nurse. This inaugural feeding was critical; the colostrum, rich with life-sustaining antibodies, was their first and most important meal to kick-start their immune systems.

Sitting in for a few more hours, Art watched over the newborns, attentive to any signs of distress or complications. His face wore a contented smile as he observed the eight brown puppies two girls and six boys finding their way to their mother's belly. The puppies' coats were so soft and wavy, with a beautiful, rich choc Ampirical Process Map olate color that reminded you of the coziest blanket you could snuggle up with on a cold winter's day. Their tiny forms clung to Lucy, who eagerly nursed them as life's first chapter unfolded before them.

Art had already fitted them with their first collars tiny bands of different colors. These were more than mere identifiers; each color was a commitment to the individual care and attention each puppy would receive under his expert eye.

As the symphony of soft whimpers and satisfied slurps filled the space, Art reveled in the sight before him generations of knowledge and decades of dedication culminated in the nurturing tableau that encapsulated his life's work. Eight new lives, each with a future as a hunting companion, began their journey under the caring watch of Art.

Art had embarked on a familiar yet always unique journey with the arrival of Lucy's new litter. During the first delicate week of their lives, Art watched over the slumbering forms of the puppies with a seasoned gaze, knowing that their world was entirely circumscribed by the warm underbelly of their mother and her nurturing presence. Lucy was their world feeding, cleaning, and warming them with an effortless grace born of instinct. Art's role was to observe and ensure that Lucy herself remained unstressed and comfortably fulfilled her maternal duties.

The barn was filled with the tender symphony of puppyhood soft nursing sounds interspersed with periods of quiet rest. These were peaceful days, moments captured in the tranquility of nurturing life. By the end of that initial week, the pen began to resonate with new sounds whines and yelps as two inquisitive pups started to crawl, their leg muscles strengthening with each ungainly movement. Art witnessed Lucy tenderly attending to their needs, stimulating their tiny bodies to function correctly with her gentle licks and nudges.

As days turned into two weeks, another milestone approached. The puppies' eyes, tightly closed, gradually began to open to the muted light of their straw-lined world. With vision came the burgeoning curiosity, and before long, they were wobbling on uncertain legs, embarking on their first unsteady explorations a testament to life's indomitable impulse.

Transitioning into the third week brought palpable changes. Energetic bursts punctuated the once calm pen, prompting Art to expand their enclosure. He constructed a space where Lucy could retreat from her boisterous offspring, affording her respite while allowing the puppies room to explore and play further. Observing their interaction with the environment and one another was among Art's simple pleasures. Even in their tenuous attempts at play, the seeds of their personalities were sprouting a joyous spectacle to behold.

As the puppies approached the one-month mark, Art recognized the importance of broadening their world to include human contact beyond just him. He invited his family to share in the nurturing process. Eager hands reached for the wriggling balls of fur, giggles, and soft words enveloping the barn. Each puppy was cradled and fussed over, with Art's gentle reminder that no pup should be left upheld; every one deserved to be showered with affection.

They were delightful, filled with uncontainable energy and a mischievous spirit that echoed through the homestead. Their tiny paws danced on the gravel, crushing fallen leaves, joyfully chasing one another in playful circles. Woofs of pure delight reverberated through the air as their wagging tails showed the sheer happiness they had brought one another. The puppies ventured into the sprawling farmland surrounding the homestead, their delicate paws tickled by the vibrant green grass. A gentle breeze whispered its secrets into fluffy ears as the pups left a trail of tiny paw prints behind as if making their magical journey. Two puppies could detect even the tiniest hidden treasures buried beneath the Earth's surface with a nose that seemed to possess superhuman capabilities. They would follow their noses with unwavering determination, like fearless explorers embarking on a daring mission, unearthing secret possessions unknown to anyone else.

The days rolled by, each bringing a discovery as the puppies grew, their bodies and senses maturing. With six weeks on the horizon, Art's veterinarian friend made his visit another appointment woven through years of mutual respect and camaraderie. The vet's eyes lit up at the sight of the vibrant little creatures before him, lively and hale.

"They have been an easy litter, and Lucy has been a great mother, something that I am always worried about when it's their first litter," Art explained, his voice tinged with pride and relief. The vet's hands were practiced and gentle as he examined each puppy, confirming their robust health before administering the vaccinations that would shield them from disease.

As the vet worked, he couldn't help but share Art's sentiments, vocalizing his admiration, "What a beautiful litter you have here, Art." They were words of simple truth, as evident in the lively pups' gleaming coats and vivacious spirits as in Art's quiet smile of satisfaction. Each had been cared for and nurtured with a devotion that paid homage to the rich tradition of breeding OK hunting dogs and lifelong companions.

As the day passed, the puppies' playful nature only blossomed, and their bond with each sibling became invaluable. They formed an unbreakable pack, unwaveringly loyal to one another within the confines of their little corner of the world. The vast fields became their playground as some chased after birds and rabbits. Their boundless energy propelled them effortlessly over fallen branches and logs, their fluffy coat disguising the uncanny agility they possessed. They would leap into the air in moments of liberation, defying gravity with each graceful bounce.

Art surveyed his estate with a sense of anticipation threading through him. Over the years, hunters drawn by his reputation had come to rely on the precision with which Art matched puppies to prospective owners. With Lucy's litter frolicking at his feet, it was time to discern which among them harbored the latent potential to excel in the hunt and which would be more suited to the role of a cherished pet.

Working as a breeder, Art had refined a meticulous approach to evaluating prospective hunting dogs. It was an intricate dance of observation and interaction, where physical vigor melded with mental acuity to single out the likely candidates. Art watched them in varied settings from the cloistered confines of the barn to the expansive and beckoning outdoors. He looked for eagerness and acumen, taking note of their alertness and curiosity, their nimble strides exuding a burgeoning boldness that the makings of a good hunting dog required.

The yard outside the barn, a swath of vibrant green, served as Art's open-air studio. Here, under the wide sky, he would watch them play, assess their temperaments, their stamina. It was a place where their nascent traits could be unfurled, where keen noses could twitch in the thrill of discovery, and bodies could be bound with an inherent understanding of the land.

Two decades had shaped Art's expertise, and he felt an affinity for the nuanced insights the Volhard Puppy Aptitude Test (PAT) offered. This battery of trials aimed to untangle the weave of each puppy's dispositional threads, revealing not just the animal's present state but shedding light on the potentiality of their future demeanor essential factors, particularly for those destined for the discipline of the hunt.

Yet already, two of the fledglings seemed less suited to the rigors and demands of the hunt. It was not a deficiency no, Art knew well the value of a dog whose destiny lay along a gentler path, companions destined for the hearth rather than the field.

For the six promising pups, Art's regimen was a series of targeted exercises drawn from the PAT and his extensive experience. They showed general promise their temperaments aligned with the ancestral call of the hunt. Among the litter, though, the puppy with the purple collar was an outlier an embodiment of the raw, appealing spirit that caught Art's practiced eye.

The little one was the epitome of amiability, approaching people with a spirited air, his tail an exuberant pendulum. Holding him sparked no revolt; he accepted touch with an easy grace, his passivity dispelling any notion of excessive assertion.

Sound did not faze him; he met it, acknowledged its existence, and recalibrated swiftly, secure once the depths of the disturbance had been plumbed and deemed harmless. The novelty of a new environment did little to dampen his spirit; he may have appeared a touch ungainly in his chaotic embrace of all directions, but he was energy unspoiled by reticence. Art had observed his keen attention to the birds that dotted their skies, an attention that preceded even Art's own awareness.

In the symphony of scampering paws and playful growls that filled Art's yard, one particular melody always stood out: the determined dash of the purple-collared pup in pursuit of any object cast into the sea of green. With an insatiable zest, this little one transformed the mundane act of retrieving into an art form.

His enthusiasm for the game was unparalleled. When a toy was sent spiraling into the air, his little body tensed, a coiled spring ready to unfurl. His eyes were sharp and focused like those of a seasoned hunter. With an explosive burst of energy, he was off, bounding through the grass with a single-minded determination that set him apart from his littermates.

There was an almost joyous tenacity in how he chased down the toy. His tiny legs would propel him across the terrain, undeterred by the distractions that captivated the others. It didn't matter where the toy would land in the thick of the brambles or across the furrowed lines of a field his commitment to retrieval was undying.

Arriving at the location, whether through instinct or the pure bliss of the chase, he would unearth the toy from its landing spot. His tiny jaws would wrap around it with a prideful gentleness, ensuring no harm came to his prize. Then, with head held high and the treasure securely in his grip, he would trot back triumphantly to Art's waiting hands. Every return was a small victory parade, a moment of success written in the wagging of his tail.

The game's allure was ceaseless for him, and if left to his own devices, it was clear this puppy would happily exhaust hour upon hour in this delightful pursuit. His indefatigable spirit was a trait that spoke of more than mere play; it hinted at the making of a remarkable companion in the field, one whose love for fetching would one day seamlessly transition into the retrieval of the game.

He was unique not only in his love for the game but in his proficiency. While his siblings might occasionally wander off course or lose interest, the purple-collared pup was unfazed, invariably homing in on the target with an efficiency that bordered on instinctual. In a brood of lively contenders, he silently claimed the crown of the consummate retriever, his every action whispering the promise of a stellar hunter in the making.

It was clear that this little one harbored the soul of a hunter, a match not just to the task but to the heart of it as well. And so, when a family patient, in anticipation, received Art's message that he had found their ideal hunting companion, it was with a sense of fulfillment that Art promised them the puppy with the purple collar. He had seen many matches made under his watchful gaze, but there was always a singular joy in presenting a talent as straightforward as this one a pleasure that never dimmed, a lineage of excellence that continued to grow.

As the day neared for the new families to arrive at the farm and collect their wagging bundles of joy, a visit from the veterinarian was in order a final health check to ensure that each puppy, including the one who bore the unique purple collar, was in perfect shape to start their new life adventure.

The veterinary truck rolled up the dusty driveway in the early morning haze, its arrival heralding a critical moment. The vet stepped out, his medical bag in hand, filled with all the tools of his trade, ready for the meticulous task awaiting him. As he entered the area where the puppies were romping, his gaze was drawn instantly to the vibrant eyes of the purple-collared puppy. They shone with an almost humanlike clarity, a deep brown-yellow hue that gleamed with intelligence and promise. The vet often thought that you could sense a puppy's zest for life through the sparkle in its eyes, and this little one's eyes were practically storytelling, holding within them a wisp of mischief that set them alight.

With each puppy corralled into a quiet corner, the vet began the thorough, systematic process of ensuring their wellness. His practiced hands moved skillfully, performing the physical examinations with a gentleness that softened the clinical nature of the action. He worked swiftly, efficiently noting each vital sign taking temperatures with a digital thermometer, counting heart rates with a practiced ear to the stethoscope, and watching their chests for the steady rise and fall that would indicate calm, rhythmic breathing.

The examination of the ears was approached carefully as the vet peered into each canal, looking for any redness, inflammation, or the shadows that mites or infection might cast. Satisfied with the cleanliness and health found there, he moved on to those captivating eyes. With a penlight, he shone a light into their depths, checking for consistent pupillary response and ensuring that the clear, glistening sheen was as much a sign of health as it was of beauty.

One by one, the vet checked all other vital body systems. He listened intently to the firm, regular beat of their little hearts and the peaceful sigh of their lungs. He palpated their abdomens, gently feeling for any signs of abnormality. Their musculoskeletal systems were evaluated with a series of flexes and stretches searching for any hints of dysplasia or joint issues.

Turning his attention to the puppies' exteriors, he examined their skin and coat running his hands through the fur to feel for any bumps or parasites lurking unseen. Each puppy was a testament to healthy living; their coats were glossy, their skin was free of irritation, and their bodies were well-formed and energetic.

Satisfied with everyone's healthy state, the veterinarian could see that the puppies were ready to leave for their new homes ready to provide comfort, joy, and companionship to those who awaited them. He could leave the farm at peace, secure in the knowledge that he was sending off a cohort of puppies that were as healthy and vibrant as they come.

Art took the responsibility of breeding and selling his prized hunting dogs seriously, ensuring his precious puppies only went to homes that would cherish and understand them, especially considering their specialized training and skills in hunting. Known for breeding exceptional hunting dogs, Art had established a sterling reputation among hunting enthusiasts. Prospective owners knew that obtaining one of Art's puppies was a privilege, often following lengthy waiting periods. Indeed, it was not uncommon for eager hunters to patiently wait for several months or even upward of a year to have the chance to bring one of Art's puppies into their homes.

The initial step involved a comprehensive application process for those interested in becoming the proud owner of one of Art's dogs. Each applicant was carefully screened through this process. Art committed himself to this thorough evaluation by consulting various professional contacts such as veterinarians and trainers. His goal was to determine the potential buyer's suitability based on their background, experience with dogs, and their proficiency in handling hunting breeds.

In one particularly memorable instance, a family showed a keen interest in adopting one of Art's puppies. The Mortis family had already established a connection to Art, as they had a relative who had previously been fortunate enough to acquire a dog from Art's renowned lineage. Having waited over eight months, the family had been promised one of the puppies. Through his diligent research, Art learned about the family's composition and their history with hunting. Mortis's parents had two children: a fourteen-year-old son and a twelve-year-old daughter. Once an avid bird hunter, the father had put his passion on hold to focus on family life. Now, with their son reaching an age suitable for learning hunting skills, the family was seen as an excellent match for a new puppy ready to undertake the role of companion and hunting partner.

After reaching out and discussing it with the family's veterinarian, Art gained insights into the family's care for animals, their lifestyle, and how they might integrate a new dog into their home. The conversations painted a picture of a responsible and loving family keen to introduce the disciplined energy of a hunting dog into their dynamic.

Convinced of the Mortis family's suitability, Art identified the perfect puppy for them. Among his litter was the spirited puppy with the purple collar, distinguishing it from its siblings. Art believed this puppy held the potential to be an ideal companion for Mortis's son, given that the boy was on the precipice of diving into the world of hunting, growing, and learning alongside.

Chapter 2

Stevie's Sightlessness

The adorable eight-week-old purple-collared puppy had captured the hearts of the Mortis family, who had been searching for their future hunting dog and companion.

"The purple-collar puppy was born to be a great hunter; his hunting instincts are superb. You are going to be very happy with him. Of all the puppies in the litter, he is the one that has a better nose," the breeder said with an enthusiastic voice.

Filled with excitement and happiness, the family could not wait to embark on a memorable journey with their newest member. The family's car hummed softly as it wove its way down the familiar roads leading from Art's farm toward the place the spirited puppy with the purple collar would soon come to know as home. Inside the vehicle, the atmosphere was abuzz with the easy chatter and laughter that often accompanies new beginnings. Held snugly in the son's lap, wrapped delicately in a soft blanket, the little bundle of fur seemed to regard the world passing by with curious, bright eyes.

Like invisible threads weaving through the car's air, names were carefully spoken and considered. Each suggestion seemed to hang as if waiting for the pup to signal his approval or voice a playful objection.

"I think that his name should be Hunter because he is going to be our hunting partner!" the mother declared with a smile, watching the little one's ears perk up as if in recognition. She saw an embodiment of their family's outdoor legacy in him: a future of crisp mornings, companionship in the silent woods, whispered praises, and the soft rustling of underbrush.

Amid the hum of the road and the murmur of the wind, the family tossed around more names, each member championing their preference with lighthearted banter. The father joked about classic dog names, the son brought up heroes from his favorite books and movies, and the daughter considered the names of grand mountains that promised adventure.

The name "Hunter," however, circled back time and again in their discussions, its suitability growing more apparent with each mention. It was a name that seemed to resonate with the spirit of the purple-collared pup a name that heralded the kind of bond that forms in the quiet companionship between a dog and his human friends out in the wilderness.

As miles turned into memories of the road traveled, the family's conversation became a comfortable consensus. It was as if the name knew its place and purpose, settling like a gentle affirmation of the pup's presence in their lives. "Hunter," they finally agreed, was indeed the perfect fit.

And so, by the time the car coasted into the driveway of their house, the consensus had taken the form of certainty. The little dog with soft brown eyes gleaming with a curious light would be called Hunter a name that spoke of his future, his place within the family, and the adventures that awaited them all.

As the family arrived home, they took their puppy, Hunter, to the front yard on a leash to relieve himself. The family knew Hunter needed to pee, especially after a long car ride, because puppies have small bladders. Following them without any issues, Hunter did indeed relieve himself. After allowing him to explore the surroundings, it was time to take him inside the house.

However, Hunter had a little stumble when they reached the four steps leading up to the front porch. Despite this, he followed the family, albeit in a peculiar jumping manner. One of the kids noticed this and pointed it out to the mother, expressing amusement at Hunter's unique way of tackling the stairs.

Inside the house, the mother decided to keep Hunter on a leash while familiarizing him with his new environment. The boy led Hunter around the house, and during their tour, Hunter accidentally placed his front paw in the water bowl the mother had just set up. The boy found this amusing and quickly dried Hunter's paw before continuing the exploration. Hunter also showed interest in the toys scattered on the floor, creating the impression that he was simply being silly and not paying attention.

When it came time to go upstairs, the boy opted to carry Hunter, considering him too young to navigate the stairs alone. In the boy's room, he released Hunter to play and got down on the floor to interact with him on a closer level. However, as the boy called Hunter, the puppy seemed to bump into him, only partially attentive to where he was going. Although the boy found Hunter's behavior odd, he didn't dwell on it and enjoyed playing with the pup. Eventually, Hunter cozily fell asleep in the boy's lap.

As the family gathered for dinner, the boy woke up Hunter. He took him outside to ensure he went to pee before joining everyone at the table. Noting that puppies typically need to relieve themselves after waking up, the boy proactively took Hunter out first. They decided to keep Hunter on a leash during dinner to prevent him from roaming around. However, Hunter bumped into the table and legs of chairs without seeming bothered by it.

Observing Hunter's behavior, the mother decided to place him in his comfortable crate in the living room instead. After whimpering, Hunter found solace in chewing one of the toys placed inside the crate. At the dinner table, the boy brought up his observations about Hunter's unusual behavior compared to their previous puppies. In response, the mother explained that Hunter had grown up on a farm and had never experienced a house environment. She assured the boy that, with time, Hunter would adjust and become a wonderful dog.

When the boy mentioned that Hunter didn't seem to be looking at them and appeared lost in his gaze, the mother proposed that Hunter might not have known who to focus on, resulting in a detached expression. She made various excuses to explain Hunter's atypical behavior, attributing it to his new surroundings.

The following day, the young boy adamantly claimed that Hunter seemed disoriented and was constantly bumping into furniture throughout the house. Concerned, the mother observed Hunter's eyes and found them to be clear and beautiful, showing no signs of any issues. She mentioned that Hunter had been given a health certificate confirming his excellent health to reassure her son.

However, the son's intuition turned out to be correct when Hunter walked past the wide balcony fence and continued, seemingly unaware of their elevated position. It was as if Hunter couldn't perceive they were on a balcony. Luckily, Hunter was securely attached to a leash and harness, preventing him from going any farther. They promptly carried him back to safety.

This incident validated the boy's observations and raised concerns about Hunter's condition despite his appearance of good health. The family now faced the task of figuring out the cause of Hunter's unusual behavior and seeking proper care and assistance for him.

It was undeniable; the pup seemed remarkably different from any other puppies they had encountered before. The family was perplexed, unable to pinpoint precisely what made Hunter stand out in such an unusual manner.

Faced with deep concern and confusion, the family knew they couldn't ignore the signs and decided to seek professional advice. Without wasting a moment, they hurriedly bundled Hunter into their car and drove toward their veterinarian clinic. The urgency in their actions radiated the love they felt and their determination to uncover the mystery surrounding their beloved pup.

The anxious car ride filled the family's thoughts with hope and anticipation. They yearned for answers that would shed light on Hunter's unusual behavior, allowing them to provide the comfort and care their furry friend needed. As the wheels screeched to a halt outside the veterinary clinic, a glimmer of optimism mingled with their worry, knowing that the expertise of their veterinarian could provide the clarity they sought.

As they entered the waiting room, their hearts pounded. They were brimming with trepidation and the desire for resolution. With Hunter in their arms, they watched expectantly as the veterinarian approached, ready to unravel the enigma surrounding their dear pup. The visit to the clinic was not just about receiving a diagnosis; it was about unlocking a deeper understanding of Hunter's needs. The family hoped this visit would yield insights enabling them to comprehend Hunter's distinct personality and provide the care and support he deserved.

The waiting room buzzed with a mix of anxiety, anticipation, and prayers for a positive outcome. In their hearts, the family knew that whatever the diagnosis might be, their love and devotion would guide them in making the best decision for Hunter's well-being. They were determined to be Hunter's support system, championing his happiness and ensuring every step of his journey was filled with love and understanding.

Hunter bounded into the examination room with contagious energy, wagging his tail and looking around. The family explained that their new puppy, Hunter, had exhibited unusual behavior after they had taken him home. With empathy in her heart, the veterinarian, Dr. Valentin, assured them she would examine Hunter and do everything she could to help him. She took a moment to observe Hunter as he excitedly explored the room. Hunter's movements were confident and agile. Dr. Valentin gently approached Hunter, getting down to his level to establish trust.

The veterinarian carefully picked up Hunter and placed him on the examination table. She began her thorough assessment by checking Hunter's weight, temperature, and vital signs. With the initial evaluation completed, the veterinarian focused on Hunter's eyes. His eyes appeared bright, clear, and beautifully colored, showcasing the familiar sparkle of a healthy pup. Despite the eyes looking healthy, the veterinarian performed a series of tests to determine Hunter's visual ability. She placed Hunter back on the floor and left the room to bring out a colorful array of toys. She waved them in front of him, observing his reaction closely. Hunter was not moving in perfect sync with their movements. At that moment, the veterinarian suggested to the family that Hunter could be blind and that she needed to perform some more eye tests to confirm his blindness. She used various specialized tools to conduct a detailed examination of the eyes. After a thorough assessment, the veterinarian explained to the family that Hunter would likely be blind.

Dr. Valentin had a diagnosis in mind, but she was still determining whether it was correct. She suspected Hunter was suffering from Sudden Acquired Retinal Degeneration Syndrome (SARDS). However, she added that it could be another eye disease. As laymen, the family was unfamiliar with these medical terms and looked puzzled when Dr. Valentin explained the disease.

The vet told them that SARDS is caused by a rapid and profound loss of function in the retina's photoreceptors, which capture light and enable vision. This disease typically affects middle-aged dogs, not puppies, and the exact cause remains unknown. However, her technical jargon only seemed to add to their confusion. Seeing the blank expressions on their faces, Dr. Valentin decided to break it down into simpler terms.

"If I may share an analogy," Dr. Valentin began, "SARDS is akin to a camera suddenly failing to capture images because the part that captures light (the 'retina') has stopped functioning." The only way to confirm if Hunter had SARDS was through an electroretinogram (ERG), a specialized test for evaluating retina function that she did not have the necessary equipment to perform at her clinic. She recommended consulting an animal ophthalmologist for a definitive diagnosis.

However, there was some consolation in her explanation: SARDS, while it does lead to loss of vision, does not cause the dog any pain or discomfort. But the comforting news was marred by the unfortunate reality that there was presently no cure or treatment to reverse the vision loss caused by the disease.

The family pondered Dr. Valentin's explanation but could not understand why the breeder or veterinarian who issued the health certificate had not noticed Hunter's blindness. The son inquired, still perplexed about how Hunter's condition had been missed. Dr. Valentin explained that dogs with SARDS often have eyes that appear entirely normal even though they cannot see. Unless SARDS is suspected, such dogs might pass a routine eye examination without raising any flags.

Confusion turned to frustration, and the son asked, "How did the breeder miss it? How could they not realize that Hunter was blind or something wasn't right with him?"

Dr. Valentin replied that Hunter was born blind or lost sight shortly after birth. Since he had never known anything different, being blind was normal. After all, dogs are born with closed eyes, which only begin to open around ten to fourteen days after birth. Hunter navigated his early days like other puppies, relying heavily on touch and scent. He could feel his mother and his littermates around him, and he used his scent instincts to locate his mother for feeding. Even as his siblings began to see, Hunter continued to navigate his world using his remaining senses.

Hunter was completely comfortable in this familiar environment. However, when he moved to his new home, he had to navigate an entirely new world, which raised the family's concerns about their new pup.

Dr. Valentin ended her explanation on a heartening note: "What's beautiful about Hunter is that he isn't frightened of exploring unfamiliar territories. On the contrary, like any other puppy, he appears full of curiosity."

Dr. Valentin emphasized that Hunter's other senses were intact, allowing him to adapt and live a fulfilling life with some supportive care. However, this news saddened the family, and the devastating truth shattered their dream of a "normal" life with their furry companion. Their expectations were now clouded by the realization that Hunter faced substantial challenges.

What struck them amid their distress was Hunter's exceptional resilience and determination. Despite his blindness, he had adapted remarkably well in his first two months of life. The family stood in awe of his strength and unwavering spirit.

However, as the family returned home, they gradually realized the demanding nature of caring for a blind puppy. They noticed subtle differences in Hunter's behavior compared to their other dogs, leading them to question how they could provide him with optimal care and support. Overwhelmed by the complexities of their situation, uncertainty, and apprehension consumed their thoughts.

Acknowledging their limitations and the challenges of caring for a blind puppy, the family faced a heart-wrenching decision. With heavy hearts, they realized that returning Hunter to the breeder was in his best interest. Tearfully, they said farewell, their hopes for a shared future replaced by a profound sense of loss. With sadness, the mother took Hunter back to the breeder. When she arrived at the farm, the breeder met her and Hunter.

"What's going on with the puppy? Why do you want to return him to me?" asked the breeder.

"Hunter is blind; our veterinarian suspected he has Sudden Acquired Retinal Degeneration Syndrome," the mother told the breeder. "We don't know how and feel uncertain how to help Hunter. We thought that it was best to return him to you," she said with sadness.

"I am glad you brought him back to me; I will try my best to help the little one," the breeder told the mother with some insecurity.

Art had always seen the bloom of remarkable potential in the purple-collared puppy. His days were often filled with observing the subtle cues and behaviors that separated a good hunting dog from a great one. So, when the news arrived, it settled upon him with the weight of unripe fruit falling before its season a tangible disappointment in the quiet space of his study, where he often retreated to contemplate the futures of the dogs he raised.

It was in the tilt of the pup's head, the eagerness in its step, and the way it seemed to attune to the sounds of nature that Art's belief had been rooted. The puppy had shown a natural ability that extended beyond the playful frolics of its siblings. It had been an essence captured in moments of serene connection with the world around him a promising whisper that spoke of fields bathed in dawn's light and the silent affirmation of a bird well retrieved.

But the unexpected news, tinged with a soft edge of reality, told a different story. The family who had taken Hunter home had other reflections to share.

In this narrative, the pup was less the hunter and more the guardian and playmate possessing a sensitivity and gentleness that, while admirable, diverged from the path Art had envisioned. The family had spoken with adoration for the puppy's warm and friendly nature, traits undeniably precious but ones that painted a portrait quite unlike the rugged silhouette of a seasoned hunting companion.

Weathered from years of molding young dogs into champions of the hunt, Art's hands trembled slightly with the weight of his reflection. He had poured knowledge and passion into raising Hunter, delicately nurturing what he believed were the inborn traits of a hunting prodigy. To hear that the pup's heart strayed from the thrill of the hunt struck a chord of dissonance in the symphony of his expectations.

Disappointment, a rare and somber guest, had visited, inviting Art to sit awhile with the shades of what might have been. Yet as the emotion made itself known, Art also felt the familiar stir of resilience that innate understanding that each dog, like a work of Art, would find its place in the tapestry of life, hunter or not. With a quiet sigh, Art rose from his chair, his eyes lifting to the expanse of land that had witnessed many such revelations, his spirit steadying itself on the promise of tomorrow.

The experienced and knowledgeable breeder found himself once again at a crossroads. Uncertain about how to proceed, he felt a profound responsibility to find the most suitable environment for the special-needs puppy. The weight of this responsibility rested heavily on his shoulders as he tried to devise an ingenious plan to help Hunter. Confusion mingled with determination as he sought to provide the blind pup with the love and care he deserved.

Hunter's journey had taken an unexpected turn, but with the breeder's determination to help him, Hunter's future was still in good hands.

Chapter 3

Stevie's Lifeline

The breeder stood in the farmyard, observing Hunter's boundless energy and playful nature. He had expected signs of struggle or at least some sort of difficulty, but there were none.

He observed with awestruck wonder as Hunter navigated his surroundings with a proficiency that belied his condition. The breeder found himself mystified, bordering on disbelief, at how a puppy with such a significant disadvantage could trot around his familiar environment with such assertive confidence.

The diminutive creature seemed to radiate an unseen aura, subbing for the mismatching sensory input with an internal guiding mechanism that allowed precision maneuvering around any obstacles that he encountered. This uncanny ability misdirected the breeder, providing a plausible reason for his initial failure to recognize or even suspect Hunter's blindness. While admiring Hunter's positivity about life, he pondered the best path forward for the young Hunter.

"Hunter, slow down! You're going to exhaust yourself," the breeder called out, watching the pup dart around the yard. "I want to find the best home for you, somewhere that understands your needs."

He recognized the importance of finding a suitable environment where his unique needs could be met with expertise and compassion. Realizing he needed assistance navigating Hunter's future, the breeder proactively contacted the English Cocker Spaniel Rescue Organization.

Art had always been meticulous when it came to the welfare of his dogs. He believed that a reliable and compassionate rescue organization would be best suited to help find Hunter a new home where his needs would be met with the utmost care and attention. Art's trust in such organizations wasn't misplaced; his own veterinarian, a professional whose opinion he held in high regard, had spoken positively about the English cocker spaniel rescue group, renowned for its excellent work in canine welfare.

This particular organization was celebrated for its attentiveness and rigorous process in the placement of dogs. They didn't simply find any home for the dogs in their care but sought the right home. Dogs under their protection were placed in thoroughly vetted foster homes, providing a temporary sanctuary where the animals could thrive until a suitable, permanent adoptive family was found. What truly resonated with Art was the organization's stringent adoption policies. They were incredibly selective and maintained high standards for potential adopters, ensuring that each of their foster dogs would go to an environment where they were loved, respected, and properly taken care of.

Impressed by their reputation and reassured by his veterinarian's endorsement, Art was inclined to seek their assistance for Hunter. He admired their commitment to matching dogs with suitable families. He was hopeful that Hunter would find a home deserving of his companionship through their extensive network and diligent screening process.

With this resolve, Art planned to reach out to the organization. He intended to call and discuss Hunter's unique personality, needs, and circumstances to understand how the rescue could facilitate the transition to a new, loving home.

Understanding the importance of this decision for Hunter's future and his peace of mind, Art was ready to take this significant step, trusting that the rescue organization would handle Hunter's case with the same dedication and care they had shown for so many other dogs in need.

Art called the rescue organization. "Hello, I have a blind pup named Hunter that needs your help. Despite Hunter's blindness, he possesses an infectious spirit, brimming with energy, cheerfulness, and fearlessness, challenging my preconceived notions of a dog's capabilities despite its sightlessness. His unexpected independence leaves me stunned and deeply inspired. As a busy farmer, however, I'm consumed by various demanding tasks and simply lack the necessary time to ensure Hunter's continued safety. While Hunter's abilities to expertly navigate his surroundings and his vibrant positivity are admirable, I find that I'm not equipped with the experience or the available hours to simultaneously ensure his safety and happiness. Hunter's well-being is paramount and deserves the dedication and focus my current lifestyle cannot provide," the breeder explained over the phone. "I want to ensure he finds a suitable environment where his unique needs can be met with expertise and compassion."

Upon receiving the breeder's plea for support, the rescue organization immediately sprang into action.

"We can assist you with Hunter," the organization representative said empathetically. "We specialize in helping English cockers like him. Our volunteers are dedicated to finding loving forever homes where dogs like Hunter can truly thrive."

The rescue organization's network of compassionate individuals joined forces and locked in their resolve to provide Hunter with the care and attention he deserved.

"We need to make sure Hunters end up in the right hands," one volunteer said with determination. "Let's tap into our network of experienced volunteers who understand the specific needs of English cockers. Together, we can secure a brighter future for Hunter."

Inside the cozy meeting room of the English cocker spaniel rescue, ornate with pictures of animals that had found new homes, a group of volunteers convened, each brimming with genuine care for the creatures they tended to. The conversation danced from topics of recent rescues to discussing the fates of their newest charges. It was here, among compassionate hearts, where the topic of the little brown puppy emerged blind since birth but charmingly vivacious.

The volunteers swaddled this puppy with particular affection, ensuring that his blindness never hindered him from feeling the full warmth of human love. His coat, a lustrous shade of chestnut, appeared to cloak him in an aura that glowed with his gentle disposition. The name *Hunter* had been bestowed upon him by the family, but as the volunteers exchanged glances, a thoughtful look crossed the face of one with a penchant for music, his thoughts harmonizing with a name born from inspiration.

As he held the little one, feeling the puppy's trust manifest in the tender nuzzle against his hand, a new name surfaced, emblematic of the pup's condition and the joy and wonder he inspired in everyone he met. "I believe 'Stevie Wonder' would be a more befitting name," he suggested, his voice carrying a blend of affection and respect for the legend whose music touched the world.

Stevie Wonder, the name of the prodigious musician who, despite his own blindness, crafted melodies that escaped the confines of the visible world, lent itself as an ideal name. The volunteer elucidated that calling the puppy Stevie Wonder would celebrate the pup's potential to overcome challenges and his special ability to bring people together much like the musical icon himself.

Indeed, it seemed perfect. With his unseeing eyes, the little brown puppy appeared to navigate the world with a kind of inner vision a sense of wonder that perhaps only those who perceive the world through different senses can truly possess. The name resonated with the volunteers, linking the puppy to a legacy of boundless talent and irrepressible spirit, reflecting an optimism that would encourage his future family to look beyond his blindness and see his extraordinary capabilities.

The conversation in the room blossomed into smiles and approving nods. *Stevie Wonder* was not just a playful homage but a badge of honor, symbolizing hope, resilience, and the boundless joy this special puppy would carry into his forever home. It was an affirmation that he, like his eponym, would not be defined by his limitations but would be celebrated for how he would undoubtedly enrich the lives of those around him.

With a resilient sense of purpose, the rescue organization's dedicated volunteers began taking Stevie under their care. They knew their primary objective was finding him a loving forever home where he could flourish. A glimmer of hope would soon replace Stevie's uncertain fate, a journey toward happiness and fulfillment.

Words about Stevie's remarkable journey spread within the rescue organization. People began sharing his story. However, days turned into weeks, and weeks became months as they tirelessly searched for the perfect forever home for Stevie. Each time someone expressed interest, they had the opportunity to meet him and witness his remarkable spirit firsthand. But as they got to know him better, they often felt overwhelmed by his boundless enthusiasm and independent nature.

They doubted whether they could handle a dog like Stevie, fearing it might be too much for them.

"He is a beautiful pup, full of life, but he is too much for us to handle him and give him what he deserves," said one of those who showed interest in adopting Stevie.

Hence, the organization continued looking for more volunteers to help find a forever home for Stevie. And then, one day, a message from a volunteer arrived that changed everything. "I found a possible foster home that could help our sweet Stevie."

Marina, a seasoned dog trainer with a commendable track record, had recently committed to expanding her unselfish efforts by applying to volunteer and provide a foster home for those in the care of the English cocker spaniel rescue organization. Her expertise extended beyond training, as she was also a certified veterinary technician, a qualification that highlighted her broad skill set and deep understanding of canine care.

Residing with her close-knit family in St. Petersburg, Florida, Marina was conveniently situated not far from the central operations of the rescue group's headquarters. This geographic proximity was advantageous for swift and efficient coordination with the organization.

At home, Marina's life was further enriched by her family, which included her husband, Joe, and their two young sons, Sean, who was eight, and Liam, age six. This lively household was no stranger to the world of dog rescue; they were already actively involved in volunteering for a bullmastiff rescue organization.

The rescue group thoroughly evaluated Marina and her family, using a standard procedure to ensure the suitability of a prospective foster home. Much to the relief and satisfaction of all involved, their application was met with approval, allowing them to join the ranks of trusted foster homes. Marina's established background in veterinary care and dog training underscored the unique assets she brought to the table.

The organization eagerly acknowledged Marina's unwavering dedication and heartfelt commitment to aiding dogs as they navigated through challenges, adapted to new environments, and often recovered from past traumas.

Given the harmonious and loving atmosphere of Marina's household and her professional qualifications, her family and home were deemed an impeccable fit for Stevie, who needed a temporary sanctuary. With specific requirements and a distinctive personality, Stevie would surely benefit from the safe, nurturing, and knowledgeable environment that Marina and her family would provide.

Marina, the dog trainer volunteer, was me. The rescue organization promptly contacted me, sharing Stevie's story and explaining the unique circumstances surrounding his blindness. The only definite information they had was his lack of sight. It was thought that he might be suffering from Sudden Acquired Retina Degeneration Syndrome, but that remained unconfirmed. The organization handling his case desired a deeper understanding of his condition to compile a comprehensive health record for him. This detailed account of his health status is critical, as it would allow potential future owners to understand his condition fully. This would ensure that he received the proper care and treatment in the future, and more importantly, it would not come as a sudden shock to his potential owners after adoption.

Perceiving the opportunity to make a difference in Stevie's life, I eagerly agreed to provide temporary shelter and care for the blind pup. Excited, I arranged a meet and greet at my house. As the volunteer arrived with Stevie, my face lit up with anticipation. Stevie, always perceptive to emotions, bounded toward me, tail wagging furiously. I crouched down, soothingly speaking to him as he sniffed my hands. "Hi, sweet boy; it looks like you and I have an adventurous journey before us."

I whispered, my voice filled with amazement; "He is even more magnificent than I thought he would be. He is a fighter, just like me. I think I can help him and make it easier to get adopted."

The volunteer who brought Stevie to me looked on, her heart swelling with happiness. It was clear that this was meant to be a perfect match between Stevie and me. The volunteer hugged me tightly.

"I believe in destiny, and it seems that destiny has brought you and Stevie together," the volunteer said, filled with emotions.

"I know you will take good care of him and know that you have an army of people cheering you on in this adventure."

Soon after, I began pouring my heart and soul into helping Stevie adapt, learn, and build confidence, ensuring that he could be ready for the subsequent stage of his life. The truth was that the special dog came to me because no one could control him.

My family and I welcomed Stevie, the foster blind dog, into our lives with a sense of joy intermingled with acute anxiety about preparing our home to ensure his comfort and safety. As a blind companion, Stevie needed a clear path to navigate while also enjoying some degree of freedom to roam around. Yet we were unsure how to properly adapt our household to our new furry friend.

I addressed my family; it felt akin to having a toddler taking their first steps. "We need to treat Stevie like a toddler who has just started walking. We should first declutter the pathways, removing any furniture that might be in the way. Remember, keeping the furniture and all other items in the same place is crucial. Changing the arrangement could disorient him and potentially cause anxiety."

With that principle established, I suggested utilizing mats with different textures. The tactile cues could indicate a new room's beginning or the stairs' start and end. These textures would serve as "signposts" for Stevie's navigation.

One of my sons chimed in, "Let's put a mat near his water bowl so he'll always know where to find it!"

I proudly acknowledged his thoughtful suggestion, replying, "That's excellent thinking!"

Next, we dedicated our thoughts to the potential risks posed by stairs. We decided to install one of the baby gates we had previously used when our children were young. Consequently, we aimed to prevent Stevie from accidentally ascending the stairs or entering certain rooms.

However, Stevie proved to be quite the adventurer. His quick learning skills and innate curiosity drove him to circumnavigate any barriers creatively. Once he discovered that the fences had a height evidenced by him stretching up and planting his front paws on the top we knew keeping his movement restricted was a lost cause. In no time, Stevie devised a method to vault over the fence.

Stevie was not content only running around the allowed parts of the house; he sought new daily challenges. He made his way up, relying solely on his paws, memory, and instinct. Stevie's fearless nature shone through as he conquered every step, each ascent a testament to his indomitable spirit. Even in the most precarious situations, Stevie displayed unwavering confidence. I still remember the first time Stevie stumbled upon a coffee table; he didn't let it deter him. Instead, Stevie quickly adapted and turned it into an obstacle course. He would hurdle over the coffee table with astonishing agility, displaying a fearlessness that astounded all who witnessed his daring acrobatics. What amazed me was Stevie's zest for life extended beyond furniture-related exploits.

Despite his antics, I looked down into Stevie's soulful, sightless eyes, puzzled over how to create a secure environment for him. "Stevie," I whispered to my courageous little explorer, "how can I transform our house into a safe haven for you, a place where you can wander freely without fear of danger?"

With human supervision not always possible, it wasn't feasible to let Stevie have free rein all the time. The solution came as a travel crate for those times when Stevie had to be left alone or needed bedtime solitude. The travel crate had solid plastic walls and a metal grate door to provide privacy and good ventilation, although giving a sense of a haunt. It became Stevie's cherished den, a cozy retreat that provided him comfort and an assurance of his safety when the human members of my family couldn't be present. The crate ensured that despite his disability, Stevie could relax, feeling secure and protected in his new home.

It felt like Stevie had an on-and-off switch; when it was on, he would go! His switch was only off when sleeping, which did not happen often during the day.

Despite some setbacks, I refused to give up on Stevie. In the meantime, I poured all my love and dedication into helping Stevie, the wild blind pup, thrive and develop his skills.

Shortly after Stevie came into my life, Stevie became a central part of my household. I had other dogs then: a fourteen-year-old English cocker spaniel named Tabu, a two-year-old English springer called Hannah, and a one-year-old bullmastiff named Petita.

For Tabu, the oldest, life had been peaceful and predictable until Stevie arrived. He could not understand Stevie's endless curiosity and boundless energy. I could see how Tabu was annoyed as Stevie interrupted his peaceful naps and romped incessantly around the house. Tabu did not wait long, and his displeasure manifested in short-tempered growls and barks whenever Stevie approached him.

It was clear that Stevie was making an effort not to encroach upon Tabu's personal space, attempting to maintain an air of calmness and tranquility. However, this indeed was a daunting task for energetic Stevie. I don't believe Stevie had a firm grasp on walking. His advances were relatively rapid; by the time Tabu's familiar scent streamed into his nostrils and sent signals to his brain, he found himself practically atop Tabu. Stevie's delayed reactions led to unavoidable confrontations. Observing such instances evoked a twinge of pity for both canines Stevie for his well-intended yet clumsy attempts and Tabu for constantly being on the verge of being bowled over.

Despite Stevie gradually learning about boundaries, the constant strain on Tabu's patience began to worry me. I was compelled to ameliorate their relationship and ease the tension. First, I decided to reintroduce Tabu's old metal crate, a haven he hadn't retired to since his puppyhood. Retrieving the crate from its neglected nook required an adequate amount of decluttering. Once cleared and thoroughly cleaned, it was prepared for Tabu's use again.

Tabu's crate was a robust metal structure lined with metal bars on all sides, allowing optimal ventilation and visibility. Placing a removable plastic tray on the floor ensured comfortable seating and hassle-free cleaning. I coddled the crate with Tabu's favorite blanket his soft spot, evident from how often he'd select it over his other blankets and cushioned the bottom with a cozy bed.

Strategically stationed in a quiet yet accessible corner, I made it explicitly clear that the crate was an open sanctuary for Tabu, permitting him to retreat there at will. Tabu quickly regained his lost attraction for his crate and acknowledged it as his inviolate fortress. On the other hand, Stevie was swiftly taught to heed this boundary, thanks to a stern warning growl from Tabu at his first curious approach toward the crate. The swiftness with which Stevie grasped this lesson was remarkable he never ventured close to the crate again.

Secondly, I declared the upstairs bedrooms exclusively for Tabu and my other dogs, thus ensuring additional safety from the boisterous Stevie. Showering Tabu with undivided affection, I reminded him that his endearing status as my companion remained unaffected. I also instituted designated solo time for Tabu, ensuring he received the much-deserved adoration and attention that had been in short supply since Stevie's arrival.

The good thing is that my other two dogs loved having Stevie around. They became Stevie's constant playmates. I remember how, on Stevie's first day with us, I took him for a leash walk (for his safety) around the courtyard, allowing him to explore and familiarize himself with his new surroundings. As I held his leash loosely, he cautiously sniffed the air, absorbing the scent of nature that enveloped him. It didn't take long before his curiosity was piqued when he detected the scent of my other dogs. I was eager to see how Stevie would interact with my dogs.

As far as I know, the initial interaction between dogs is primarily based on the powerful canine sense of smell, a process known as olfaction. Dogs often begin their encounters by detecting each other's scent from a distance, garnering vital information before proceeding to more direct contact. However, in Stevie's case, this process was far more elaborate. Being visually impaired, Stevie's ability to discern other dogs' scent signatures and pheromones from afar was critical. His heightened sense of smell provided him with preliminary insights about other dogs without needing to be in immediate proximity. His uncanny ability to bump into my other dogs, even on a leash, was remarkable.

Upon witnessing Stevie's various unlikely encounters with my other dogs, I was struck by the noticeable absence of eye contact from Stevie's end, a behavior generally expected in dog communication. Stevie had an odd way of colliding directly into my dogs, literally bumping into them, seemingly without looking. This unusual approach initially put Petita and Hannah on guard, their caution evident as they circled Stevie, attempting to attract his attention visually and gauge his reaction.

Unable to curb his excitement, Stevie responded with vivid enthusiasm. His tail was a blur of joyous wagging; perky ears were alert, attentive, and curious. His mouth was slightly opened, his happy panting almost resembling a cheerful grin. Regardless of the investigative advances of Petita and Hannah, he maintained a submissive play bow, dropping the front half of his body low while his rear end remained elevated. Gingerly, he rolled onto his back, baring his vulnerable underbelly, clearly demonstrating submissiveness and trust. His jovial and respectful behavior gradually melted their initial wariness, leading them to see him as an eccentric but harmless playmate. At this juncture, I doubt they fully comprehended Stevie's visual impairment yet.

Over time, Petita and Hannah learned to adapt their communication style to accommodate Stevie's needs, relying heavily on auditory cues like vocalizing and scratching the ground. Unfazed by his inability to see, Stevie continued to play in his unique style, decoding the energy levels of my other dogs through their panting rhythm, the intensity of their barks or growls, and their subtle movements. His uncanny ability to track the other dogs based on their paw steps, the rustle of their collars, and even their breath reminded me of how well he had adapted to his condition.

The gentle vibration of the ground beneath and the direction of the airflow also aided Stevie in ascertaining the location and movement of the other dogs. Observations of these interactions put forth the idea that Stevie could physically detect my other dogs' energy. He, in essence, felt the momentum from their high-speed antics, the rhythm of wagging tails, and the enthusiastic sounds emitted during their playful pursuits.

Meanwhile, my intelligent German shepherd, Aki, adopted a more cautious approach. A month after we began to foster Stevie, Aki came into our lives. Aki was known as a "green dog" in the context of police dogs. This term refers to a young and untrained dog with the potential for police work. Law enforcement agencies or individual handlers typically purchase these dogs and undergo rigorous training programs to become fully trained police dogs. They are trained for various purposes, such as detecting drugs and explosives or performing search and rescue operations. I planned to train Aki as a Patrol K9, a specially trained dog that works alongside law enforcement officers. Aki, a 10-month-old dog from Holland, was my new companion for this training journey.

Preferring to watch Stevie from a safe distance, Aki observed his interactions with the other dogs, patiently waiting for the right moment to interact with the new dog.

Petita, Hannah, and Stevie quickly became a sight to behold, their synchronized movements making them appear as if they all possessed the gift of sight. Their seamless coordination honed a sense of unity, a bond built on trust and understanding. Stevie's blindness became irrelevant, as his other remarkable senses allowed him to keep up with his friends effortlessly.

When my other dogs needed a little break from playing, they lay down. Lying down made Stevie understand that the other two dogs needed a break; I watched Stevie gracefully maneuver through the open space, his senses attuned to every step, every twist and turn.

As Stevie approached the vinyl fence enclosing my backyard, I felt a pang of concern. Until this point, Stevie had relied on his heightened senses of smell, touch, and hearing to navigate his surroundings. Confronting a static, substantial structure like a vinyl fence presented a new challenge for him and a tense moment for me. Yet, my concerns began to ease as I observed Stevie's tactic. As he neared the fence, his pace gradually slowed, indicating an awareness of some change in his environment.

Lowering his snout to the fence's base, he commenced a deep, investigative sniffing session, painstakingly parsing the new scent signature of the vinyl material. His careful footfalls along the fence were methodical as if he was creating a mental blueprint of the fence's expanse and physical boundaries.

Within a couple of days, Stevie's behavioral adjustment to this new fixture was remarkable. His refined senses and spatial memory had formed an accurate mental map of the fence's location. Stevie was now adept at halting his path just before the point of collision. The small changes he picked up on were impressive: the subtle shift in temperature as he neared the cooler vinyl fence, the perceived reduction in air movement associated with a solid obstacle, and the noticeable transition from the soft grass under his paws to the harder texture of ground along the fence's bottom.

Stevie deftly assimilated these precise environmental cues to avoid accidental run-ins with the fence. The few times he graze against it was not due to a failure in detection but rather an inability to halt his momentum in time. While lacking in sight, his sensory abilities enabled him to form a comprehensive "picture" of the vinyl fence.

Stevie's curiosity led him to the enticing allure of the backyard swimming pool. As he approached, I watched closely, ready to help him if he fell into the pool, something that possibly would happen. Stevie eagerly approached the pool; little did he know that the sparking blue water would present a small challenge for him. Despite his blindness, Stevie's adventurous spirit never wavered, and he drove headfirst into the pool, unaware of the lack of clarity in his aquatic surroundings. As soon as I saw Stevie falling into the pool, I yelled, "Stevie fell in the pool!" letting the rest of my family know what was happening.

Without a second thought, I dove into the pool, my heart pounding, instinct driving me to ensure Stevie's safety. As my arms closed around him, I felt his panic-stricken wriggling cease; it seemed that my touch reassured him, calming him amid the turbulent water.

Heaving him out of the pool, I observed him shake the water off, a spray of droplets shimmering in the sunlight. In the aftermath of what could have been a harrowing situation, Stevie seemed unfazed, immediately reverting to his usual carefree demeanor as if he had not just been plunged unexpectedly into the pool.

His boundless energy was at once endearing and nerve-wracking. No sooner had the first ordeal ended than Stevie, in his robust enthusiasm, dashed right back into the pool! I could hardly stifle a gasp; before I knew it, I was back in the water, swiftly hoisting the soggy ball of energy out once more.

This time, we decided to be extra cautious. I held onto the wriggling puppy tightly, ensuring he didn't slip out of my grasp for another audacious plunge. My oldest son, Sean, sprinted over swiftly with a towel. Grasping Stevie firmly, he began to rub the towel over him briskly, drying off the drenched fur while I continued to clutch onto our adventurous canine.

Sean and I exchanged glances that reflected our shared astonishment as he worked. This diminutive yet spirited pup seemed to have no concept of fear. His audacity had caught us off guard, but it was clear that we needed to remain hypervigilant with Stevie around. His innocent sense of adventure was certainly heartwarming, but it was evident that his safety quotient needed a constant watch!

However, there were other times Stevie fell into the pool; while we were at the pool, I would take a big breath, and I gently encouraged and assured Stevie I would guide him. Because I knew this could happen again, I decided it would be better not to jump into the pool to help him. I helped him find ways to get out of the pool if he fell again and no one was around.

I directed Stevie toward the pool's edge using carefully chosen words and a soothing voice.

"Stevie, I am here; come to me. I will help you to get out of the pool."

Step by step, I instructed Stevie to paddle closer to my voice. Stevie faithfully followed my guidance; he could hear my calm voice becoming louder and more evident. The water displaced by this slender body signaled his growing proximity to the pool's edge, indicating his safe arrival.

But the journey wasn't over yet. Stevie still needed to find a way to exit the pool. Quickly, I located the nearest set of pool stairs. Clapping my hands, I directed Stevie toward the steps, ensuring his path was obstacle-free.

Through patience, good communication, and unwavering support, Stevie's paws eventually found solid ground as he stepped onto the pool stairs. I reached over his collar at the stairs and helped him get out. After Stevie got out of the pool, he acted happy, wagging his tail like nothing had happened. He wagged his tail joyfully, reaffirming his trust in his human companion.

While Stevie was shaking the water off him, I told my family, "From now on, as part of his training, I will devise a plan to teach Stevie how to locate the pool's edge and find the steps for his safe exit. I will signal his attention with a clap and let him hear my location. It will become our distinctive language, a way for me to guide him in the water. I clapped when he accidentally tumbled into the pool, and Stevie immediately focused on my direction. He swam purposefully, his tail wagging energetically until he reached the pool's edge. He located the steps and elegantly climbed out there, triumphantly conquering the water's challenges. Together, we will practice finding the pool's edge and a safety exit, turning each dip into a triumph of victory."

Over time, Stevie's encounters with pools evolved from unplanned tumbles into the pool to mastery of canine aquatic etiquette. Experience and practice equipped him with the skills necessary to navigate the unfamiliar pool terrain.

He quickly developed a meticulous approach to his actions in a body of water, painstakingly aware of every move. Stevie discovered his inner canine swimmer.

He learned to paddle with a rhythm, his body buoyant and his movements swift but controlled. He oriented himself toward the pool's ledge, instinctively grasping the exit route. Feisty as he was, he began pulling himself onto the ledge, his small body straining with effort but never faltering. Stevie mastered the art of getting out of the pool independently, without the aid of a human lifeline.

His learning wasn't limited to familiar surroundings. Stevie proved his adaptability extended even to unknown territories. Even when faced with unfamiliar pools, he continued. His quick thinking and sharp senses guided him, his learning experiences aiding each new circumstance.

But, as much as he seemed capable alone, we never left it to chance. We stayed within reach each time he was near a pool. His adventurous spirit was relentless, so we were his vigilant guardians, ready to step in if his safety was compromised. As much as Stevie learned and grew, his safety remained our unwavering priority.

Because I knew the training would take time, we replaced the pool fence, which we had used when the boys were little. That would keep Stevie safe. When my family and I were by the pool without the fence, to keep Stevie safe, I purchased a floating vest designed for dogs, allowing him to experience the joy of swimming and running around the pool without worry.

Through these experiences, I witnessed Stevie's remarkable capacity to adapt and learn, his determination driving him to overcome any obstacle. It was as if his blindness had opened up new avenues of perception, heightening his senses and instilling in him an unwavering sangfroid.

The name of a professional animal ophthalmologist was handed to me by the rescue organization so I could check out Stevie. I was also intrigued and eager to find out Stevie's exact condition to ensure that there were no potential complications I wasn't aware of or, if indeed there were, to understand how it might affect his medical needs. Wasting no time, I swiftly arranged for a visit.

The excursion to the animal ophthalmologist turned out to be quite an intriguing experience. Upon arrival, we informed the vet tech of our scheduled appointment with Dr. Vista and settled into the waiting area. We were not the only ones waiting; at least five other animals, including dogs and cats, were in line for their turn. For an area filled with animals, it was surprisingly peaceful. A cursory examination of the other animals revealed noticeable eye issues, like cataracts, severe dry eye, conjunctivitis, and even a cat devoid of eyes.

On the other hand, Stevie's eyes radiated health and beauty. I felt slightly out of place. The temptation to announce Stevie's condition to everyone, that beneath those beautiful eyes lay blindness, was quite high. However, we were ushered in before I got the chance to explain. Eventually, I concluded that justifying our presence to others was unnecessary.

Dr. Vista, a youthful and pleasant veterinarian, greeted us warmly. She ran us through her plan, which included conducting some preliminary eye tests on Stevie before resorting to an electroretinogram (ERG). The ERG is a noninvasive test designed to assess the retina's response to light. However, due to Stevie's unrest, caused by an overflow of excitement from being the center of attention, Dr. Vista opted to administer a tranquilizer to calm him down before the tests. After conducting the initial checks, the vet performed the ERG test. As speculated, the test results confirmed that Stevie was afflicted with Sudden Acquired Retina Degeneration Syndrome (SARDS), a condition more common in middle-aged dogs with no known cause or cure.

Dr. Vista concluded our visit by reassuring me that Stevie was not experiencing any discomfort despite his diagnosis but forewarned that it would be crucial to monitor him for potential long-term conditions like glaucoma, which can cause severe pain.

Upon receiving the diagnosis from the veterinarian, we finally understood the precise nature of Stevie's ocular condition. This crucial information allowed us to communicate transparently with potential adopters, ensuring they fully grasped his vision. While it was disheartening to learn that Stevie's eyesight issues were irreversible and that medical intervention could not offer further assistance, there was a silver lining in our discovery: Stevie was free from pain. This knowledge brought significant relief and allowed us to focus on his quality of life rather than medical solutions.

Committed to ensuring Stevie's future, I continued with his training regimen, enhancing his skills and adaptability and increasing his chances of finding a loving, permanent home. I dedicated myself to working with him daily, employing gentle guidance, consistency, and an abundance of affection. As the days unfurled into weeks and the weeks stretched into months, my bond with Stevie grew stronger. Through our shared experiences, I observed firsthand how nurturing care and steadfast patience positively influenced his demeanor.

Stevie's resilience and trust blossomed throughout this time, further showcasing his endearing nature to all who met him. Our journey together was a profound reminder of the healing and transformative potential of love and patience when caring for needy animals. This deep connection and commitment to Stevie's well-being did not just prepare him for a new life with a forever family but also enriched my life with invaluable experiences and lessons in compassion.

Chapter 4

Stevie's Remarkable Abilities

While caring for Stevie, I began reaching out to some friends I knew had been considering adopting a dog. I had a lingering hope that they might find Stevie to be the perfect addition to their homes. Because I am a professional dog trainer, my friends were aware that if I recommend a specific dog for adoption, it is because I judge the dog to be well-behaved, gentle, and amiable.

Stevie was not only a dog I was confident in recommending but also a dog that was already conditioned to live in a home setting. Before Stevie was sent to any home, I intended to ensure he was thoroughly trained. I was offering to introduce Stevie to their lives and assist with the transition, ensuring that he would adjust perfectly.

To facilitate this, I invited my friends to come and meet Stevie personally at my house, giving them a chance to observe his behavior and interact with him. They could witness firsthand how Stevie had developed under my guidance and assess his interactions with them. In this way, they could make a more informed decision about adopting him.

The introduction of Stevie, the wondrous little canine with the heartwarming sobriquet, to my circle of friends was an occasion that sparked a constellation of reactions and emotions, mirroring the complexity of an intricate tapestry.

As we gathered in my spacious but cozy living room where the gentle hum of conversation complemented the soft creaks of well-loved wooden floorboards Stevie made his debut with a quiet charm that belied his vibrant name. Stevie navigated the space with surprising ease; his other senses tuned to the laughter and whispers that filled the room, painting a picture of his world in broad yet delicate strokes.

My friends, arrayed on plush sofas and armchairs scattered with an eclectic mix of patterned cushions, watched as Stevie acquainted himself with each new person and corner. Their initial reactions were a blend of admiration and delight at his poise and gentle manner. Joyful exhalations greeted his every successful maneuver around coffee tables and people's legs a demonstration of his manageable nature and the result of diligent training. My friends shared smiles at his well-behaved antics, the careful way he approached each of them, the unwavering tail wags, and the soft, warm presence they could feel when he lay near.

But as the afternoon ambled on, the initial veneer of simple joy began to crack, revealing layers of trepidation and practicality that adult life inevitably draws forth. Suspicions began to take root in the minds of potential adopters, growing amid their genuine fondness for Stevie.

One friend, whose life was a tightrope walk between professional demands and personal fulfillment, voiced their concerns subtly at first. They expressed an uncertain pause that as graceful as Stevie was, he was undeniably "a lot of dog" a sentiment that echoed in the nods of others. The overarching worry was not of love or desire to welcome Stevie but the quiet acknowledgment of the weighty commitment that his care would entail; the necessity for constant attention and adaptation to his special needs seemed to stretch beyond the confines of their already chock-full schedules.

For my friends with youngsters toddling about, there was a palpable tension in the joyous chaos that marked their days. The thought of integrating Stevie, a soul so sweet yet requiring guidance in a world unseen to him, seemed to add a daunting layer of complexity to the multifaceted task of parenting they were just beginning to master.

Pet parents in the group offered their perspectives too, some with a hint of resignation. They already navigated the delicate dance of interspecies relationships at home, where felines reigned and had established an intricate set of household rules that new additions would have to fit into, a puzzle that Stevie's presence was likely to complicate.

Various other apprehensions were softly murmured next to cups of half-drunk coffee, each providing a gentle but firm barrier to the potentiality of a life shared with Stevie. From allergies to space constraints, each concern was laid out with the quiet heaviness of unrealized possibilities.

In the end, as Stevie continued to grace us with his serene company, unaware of the swirling currents of human concern, there was an unspoken consensus. Love for him was ample, but the collective ability to provide the particular kind of home he needed was insufficient, much to our shared sadness. It was a realization wrapped in bittersweet acceptance.

Two months had passed since Stevie, the once-nervous dog with vision loss, had entered my life as a foster pet. During this time, my understanding of his remarkable nature had grown exponentially. Despite his inability to see, Stevie navigated the world with such confidence and determination that his blindness seemed almost inconsequential. I noted with fascination how he used his other senses to explore and interact with his surroundings; it was as if a veil had been lifted, revealing Stevie's true capabilities.

Day by day, I watched as Stevie adapted to his environment with an inspiring level of ingenuity and grace. His keen hearing, acute sense of smell, and heightened awareness of touch enabled him to map out the space around him, find his way, and build trust with those he encountered. What initially seemed like a limitation had indeed opened a new realm of potential for Stevie, and it became clear that his condition did not dampen his spirit or love for life.

Observing Stevie's fearless approach to life's challenges and his boundless positivity transformed my perspective, filling me with a profound sense of admiration and respect for his resilience. His abilities stretched far beyond what one might expect from a dog in his situation; Stevie was not just managing; he was thriving.

One quiet evening, as I sat reflecting on our journey together, a decisive thought crystallized in my mind. A deep, heartfelt recognition of the bond we had developed and the extraordinary character Stevie possessed led me to a meaningful conclusion. With a sense of certainty and a swell of affection in my heart, I whispered a promise to myself: "I am going to give Stevie a forever home and adopt him." From that moment, I knew our foster arrangement was no mere temporary situation. It was the beginning of a lifelong companionship with an incredible dog who had, without a doubt, already found his permanent place in my home and heart.

What always amazed me was Stevie's ability to navigate his surroundings, even at just six months old. Despite being blind, he effortlessly maneuvered through various environments, avoiding large objects like trees, cars, and fences without hesitation.

"Stevie, it is amazing that in known surroundings, you don't look blind! I remember that a few days after you were brought to me, you could run around the pool with Petita and Hannah as you knew perfectly where the pool was. You only fell in the pool a few times, and usually, it was because one of the other dogs pushed you accidentally. I am glad you always wore a flotation vest while running around the pool to keep you calm if you fell in," I said to him with admiration.

Watching him explore the world so gracefully was awe-inspiring and filled me with immense pride.

To help him enhance his physical abilities, I sought safe locations where he could freely run and play without limitations. Among these places, his absolute favorite was the dog beach.

He loved the feeling of the warm sand beneath his paws and the gentle caress of the ocean breeze on his fur. The first time I took Stevie to the beach, he took a deep breath, savoring the salty air, and set off on his new escapade. Stevie's excitement was palpable. Even though he couldn't see the vibrant colors of the beach, it felt like he could feel the expanse of golden sand stretching out before him. Stevie confidently explored his nose close to the ground, relying on his senses to navigate the beach.

With the sound of crashing waves, Stevie's ears perked up, trying to make sense of the unfamiliar auditory cues. He picked up on the rhythmic, repetitive sound of the tides rushing in and out, tickling the shoreline. He instinctively followed his noise, feeling the vibration of each wave against his paws as it inched closer.

Stevie kept exploring, relying on his sense of hearing, smelling the tangy scent that grew more distinct with each step. The smell of seaweed, salt, and even the occasional fish gave him a sense of the vastness before him.

Stevie felt hesitant as he reached the water's edge, sensing a sudden change in temperature as the waves lapped at his paws. The sensation of calm, gentle waves cautiously coming for him caused an uncertain wag of his tail. He might have listened to the sound of the water receding, creating a swirling, foamy sensation around his feet.

When Stevie reached the water's edge, I gently reassured him that he could keep exploring and that he was safe with me. We slowly stepped into the cool, refreshing water. I led the way and offered a steady hand for support. Stevie hesitated a little at first as we walked deeper into the water, unsure of what lay ahead. My guidance created a sense of trust between him and me. Stevie felt my sense of unwavering presence, which gave him the confidence to take the next step. We continued moving, and the water gradually deepened.

"Stevie, we are getting to the point where you must start swimming," I softly said.

With me close to him, Stevie realized that he was not walking anymore. He started to paddle with his front legs, feeling the water's buoyancy supporting his body, and then he started swimming.

"Wow, Stevie, you are swimming on your own!"

While swimming, he discovered a newfound freedom and independence. He relied on his senses as he navigated the water, especially hearing and touch. Stevie gained more confidence with every stroke, and his tail wagged in pure joy.

With his sharp sense of smell, Stevie managed to pick up the rustling sound and distinctive scent of birds nearby. A group of birds had gathered in an open space before him, and they had caught his attention.

However, the birds did not fly away when they saw Stevie approaching them. Instead, the birds started swimming away from him.

His hunting instincts matured, and Stevie didn't hesitate even for a moment. With a splash, he began swimming, paddling quickly with a determination to get closer to the birds. His strong doggie paddles create rapid ripples in the calm water. As I watched from a distance, fear gripped me.

I was worried that Stevie would overestimate his swimming ability. He was enthusiastically pursuing the birds who were adept at swimming and potentially leading him farther from the shore. I feared that Stevie could exhaust himself trying to keep up, and worse, he could be so far out that he would battle to find his way back. Not being around me, his caretaker, could add to his confusion and increase his risk of drowning.

My growing anxiety started to morph into a mild panic, and I knew I needed to act. I had to recall him, but I needed to not startle him. Alarmed or rushed commands might throw him into a panic. Therefore, trying to keep my voice steady and exuding a sense of security, I called, "Stevie, here!" I hoped that hearing my voice would orient him and prompt him to swim back toward the safety of the shore.

Then Stevie turned and faced me. "Good boy, Stevie! Keep coming in my direction. Here, Stevie. That's my boy," I kept saying while Stevie swam toward me, and we got out of the water safely.

Once he reached the shore, I swiftly wrapped Stevie in my arms. My emotions escalated, and a couple of tears managed to escape, trickling slowly down my cheeks. A multitude of emotions amplified the overwhelming rush of relief that swept through me.

A notable fear hung thickly in the air, originating from the horrifying thought of almost losing Stevie to the water. Knowing he was safe back in my arms did not fully erase the lingering fear, but it acted as a soothing balm for my frantic mind.

This coalescence of dread and relief was intertwined with profound happiness, a joy that echoed loudly in the silent background. Stevie was safe and sound, here with me. He had returned unscathed from an impromptu adventure, filling me with a warmth that finally allowed the unshed tears to roll down.

Stevie, oblivious to the emotional maelstrom his caretaker was experiencing, was brimming with a childlike satisfaction. Flooding with innocent joy, he appeared as pleased as a clam and did not seem to grasp the potential danger he had found himself in mere minutes ago.

He sat there, nestled within the familiar and comforting frame of my arms, completely oblivious to the difficult journey he had embarked upon. His ignorance of the danger only fueled my emotional rush, blending a peculiar mixture of relief, fear, and happiness.

Following that incident, a wave of self-reproach hit me. I couldn't help but question myself: how could I have been so careless? Knowing Stevie as I did, I knew he had a strong hunting instinct, especially for birds. Yet, I hadn't foreseen that his instinct could place him in such a hazardous situation.

Though it was discomforting, I began to question my previous decisions and oversight, and this self-criticism also sowed the seeds of a valuable lesson. I realized the importance of exercising more caution whenever birds were present around Stevie, particularly in proximity to water bodies.

From then on, I knew I had to be more vigilant in environments with birds. In such situations, I would keep Stevie under even closer supervision, and if required, I would use a leash to ensure his safety. The incident was enlightening, teaching me to consider and respect his instincts more and adapt my approach to ensure his safety and well-being. I decided it was enough for that day and left the beach with Stevie on the leash.

However, that day, I knew that coming to the beach to swim and chase the birds was going to be his favorite activity.

Stevie's zest for life was evident in every aspect of his being. He wholeheartedly embraced new experiences if he had the reassurance of my presence. He adapted quickly to bustling city streets or serene nature trails and approached each adventure with curiosity. What struck me the most was how his blindness didn't hinder his enthusiasm or optimism but rather heightened his reliance on his other senses, making him a true master of his surroundings.

During this period, I noticed a distinct and unusual pattern emerging in Stevie's behavior that caused me to pause and take notice. There were moments when he would break away from his typical demeanor, acting in ways that were not his norm. He would abruptly jump on me, focusing his sudden burst of energy on my face with a particular insistence that was quite uncharacteristic of him.

Stevie would hastily lick at my face, a behavior he had never exhibited before, coupled with barks echoing an unusual urgency. This unpredictable change in his conduct felt unsettling and gave me the impression that he was out of control. My immediate reaction was to regain control over the situation, so I gently but firmly placed Stevie back on the floor, holding him there to calm him down. Despite my intervention, he was persistently trying to jump up to my face again, making me question the reason behind this peculiar behavior.

What struck me as most intriguing was that these episodes of strange behavior happened to align perfectly with the time right before the agonizing onset of my migraine attacks. At first, I couldn't comprehend the possible correlation between the two seemingly unrelated events.

However, after another similar incident occurred, a striking revelation hit me. I began to connect the dots, leading me to an astonishing deduction: Stevie was actually sensing the aura that often precedes my migraines. His out-of-character behavior was in response to these impending attacks. He was able to detect the subtle changes in me that indicated an approaching migraine, and he was trying to alert me in his unique way. This realization was surprising and cast Stevie's peculiar behavior in an entirely different, empathic light.

As a young adolescent, I was plagued by the excruciating condition known as Status migrainosis. This type of severe migraine is typified by an unbearable headache that is both persistent and debilitating, refusing to relent for an agonizing stretch of seventy-two hours. It's akin to being struck powerfully by a baseball bat, following which your head feels as though it's clamped tightly in a vice. Even the slightest shift or movement seems to amplify the pain. In essence, Status migrainosis left me perpetually exhausted and sapped me of emotional resilience. The chronic pain frequently disrupted my life, turning routine into the extraordinary.

"Stevie, you are amazing, and you came into my life for a reason! Knowing that with your help, I can take vital precautions to avoid having those awful headaches, my life will change positively," I told him with a smile on my face.

Realizing the immense potential that Stevie possessed, I made a life-changing decision. I couldn't ignore that he had become an integral part of my life and had a unique ability to assist with my migraines. With his keen senses, intelligence, and unwavering loyalty, training him as my service dog seemed to like the natural next step. He would not only help me before my migraines but also provide support by helping me to be prepared and take necessary precautions.

It was a typical evening, with the house cloaked in the tranquil silence that only comes when the world is adrift in the sea of dreams. The night had folded itself around us like a velvet shawl, and the steady breaths of my son in the next room were a quiet testament to the peace that had settled within our walls. Stevie had claimed a cozy nook at the foot of my son's bed, a sentinel even in slumber. There was something almost spiritual in the bond he shared with Liam, a connection that extended far beyond the spoken word into the realm of silent understanding.

But this particular night, as the moon climbed the arch of the heavens, a subtle shift unfurled in the tapestry of the darkness. My son's soft, hesitant footsteps approached, disrupting the rhythm of sleep's quiet ballet. His hand on my shoulder was both gentle and urgent. "Mom," he whispered, his voice a silken thread in the hush, "Stevie wouldn't stop whining. He kept nudging me until I woke up. He wants you."

The somber concern in my son's words clearly conveyed Stevie's distress. As Stevie padded into my room and up to the edge of my bed, an insistent whine escaping his throat, I could immediately feel the tense aura he exuded. Then came the gentle but insistent pawing at my arm, a message delivered with a silent but potent force. Stevie's eyes, though unseeing, seemed to gaze into my very core, discerning the tide of discomfort rising within me before even I had fully registered it a migraine looming on the edge of my consciousness like a gathering storm.

There, in the muted glow of the night light, we marveled at Stevie's extraordinary gift. His presence was a soothing balm against the creeping pain, as if he had, indeed, some mystical power.

"Wow, Stevie astonished us again with his strong senses!" I said, the words tinged with a respect that deepened with each passing day. I smiled with a mix of gratitude and wonder for the extraordinary creature before us.

"Ma, it looks like Stevie has magical powers!" my son exclaimed. His voice was ripe with youthful awe and unclouded enthusiasm.

Liam brought me my medication along with a glass of water. Feeling relieved, I was grateful to know that my sweet Stevie had preempted the migraine that was about to strike.

Our laughter, tinged with affection and amazement for our family's unlikely hero, gently perforated the quiet of the night. We showered Stevie with caresses, each touch speaking volumes of our adoration for him. As the vigilant guardian took his place beside my bed, offering his silent vigil, I couldn't help but feel that in the tapestry of life, with its myriad threads of experience, we had been woven together with this extraordinary dog in a pattern that was as beautiful as it was mysterious.

Creating a training program specially adapted for Stevie and my requirements was essential. This would entail a detailed process in which I had to identify what tasks he would be performing for me before, during, and in the aftermath of a migraine episode.

The core requirement was that Stevie had to recognize and respond correctly to the onset of a migraine. One remarkable thing was that Stevie already possessed the ability to detect the changes in my body chemistry linked with the commencement of a migraine episode by using his superior sense of smell. Dogs similar to Stevie, including those trained to detect diabetes or migraines, are typically trained using saliva. This is because saliva contains traces of certain chemicals that fluctuate when the body is about to experience a migraine or changes in blood sugar levels.

In anticipation of another migraine episode, I prepared to collect a saliva sample once I felt its onset, a process already signaled by Stevie. Extra caution was needed to ensure that the collected sample was free from contamination by any foreign scents. An essential preparation was to ensure all materials were adequately arranged prior to the collection to ensure a smooth and efficient process.

The next step of the training involved scent association, the scent of my saliva during a migraine was paired with a high-value treat, creating a linked response in Stevie's behavior. I thought about what kind of behavior I wanted Stevie to exhibit once he recognized the scent; actions like nudging, barking, staring, or licking were considered. I chose pawing as the desired reaction because that was something he never naturally did.

To get Stevie adept at pawing me whenever he detected the impending shift in my body chemistry was no simple task. In the world of dog training, this process is known as "shaping." Shaping involves breaking down the main training goal into smaller, more achievable steps. As the dog masters each step, they are rewarded, which encourages further learning. This method helps the dog to progressively learn new behaviors by connecting each successful step to a positive experience. This step-by-step process allows a dog to understand and work toward the final goal gradually. Through shaping, Stevie could learn to move progressively toward the end goal, pawing me when he detected the changes in chemistry in me.

Simultaneously, while teaching Stevie the migraine detection process, I also started training him on the action of retrieving my medication, a crucial part of coping with the pain once the migraine set in. In some instances, the headache would arrive unheralded, striking me with intense pain at once. During these times, I wanted Stevie to be capable of fetching my medicine for me. However, due to his visual impairment, a different approach was required in comparison to how visually abled dogs were trained.

To ensure that Stevie could always locate my medication, regardless of our location, because we often traveled and stayed in different places, I decided to store my pills in a secure container that would consistently be situated next to his water bowl inside a basket. This spot was ideal, given that Stevie had a natural instinct to always know where his water was located. Furthermore, while in public, his service vest had a mini container designed to carry my medication.

The whole process of teaching a dog to retrieve a specified object in this case, my medication was broken down into small steps of progression. The initial step involved training Stevie to take objects from my hand, and then the complexity was slowly increased by teaching him to pick up objects from the floor. Ultimately, he was taught to fetch objects located at a distance and bring them to me. This whole process was continued until Stevie learned to fetch my medication in response to a specific command or cue.

I developed a unique and unmistakable signal for our exceptional dog, Stevie, to communicate a specific need. The chosen cue was the distinct sound produced by me tapping the top of my head with the palm of my hand. This action generated a noise that Stevie, with his acute sense of hearing, learned to recognize amid the myriad of commonplace sounds that humans typically generate throughout the day.

Through careful and repeated training sessions, Stevie came to associate this distinctive auditory signal with an important task. He understood that the tapping sound of my hand contacting my head was an alert, a call to action signifying that it was time for me to take my medication. Upon hearing this cue, he knew precisely what was required of him.

Stevie was meticulously trained to respond to this cue by undertaking the critical responsibility of retrieving my medication. Each time I delivered the tap on my head, Stevie reacted promptly. His training had ingrained in him the knowledge that this specific sound meant his immediate assistance was needed. With this understanding, he would quickly search for and bring me the medication, thus showcasing not only his intelligence and skill but also his invaluable role in supporting my well-being.

As time passed, I began envisioning future goals for Stevie's training. One significant aspiration was to train Stevie to comfort me during the throes of a migraine attack. Ideally, he would lie next to me, his body in contact with mine, providing both physical and emotional relief while I was confined to bed, wracked by the pain.

Moreover, I also hoped to train Stevie to seek assistance from family members on command. The idea was that if I was unable to leave my bed during a severe migraine, Stevie could be sent to fetch a family member who could help me.

However, such advanced training would have to be postponed. At five months old, Stevie was young, full of energy, and still in the early stages of his education. He was not yet prepared to begin learning such complex tasks. These sophisticated skills are usually incorporated into a service dog's training schedule as they mature and polish their foundational abilities. The promise held by Stevie's youth was palpable, and his enthusiastic nature gave me the confidence that he'd soon be ready for these advanced stages of training.

An integral aspect of a service dog's training involves cultivating appropriate conduct in public places. The ideal service dog is hidden; its presence should be virtually undetectable to those around them. Hence, the need to instill good behavior in public places was crucial for Stevie's training. The first step in achieving this behavior involved thorough obedience training and comprehensive socialization.

Service dogs are typically trained in a set of basic commands like *sit-stay*, *down-stay*, *come*, *leave it*, *wait*, *place*, *off*, and *heal*. For Stevie, this standard training regimen needed to be adjusted to account for his visual impairment. Thus, it was necessary to carefully assess and choose the commands that would be most vital for Stevie to learn and understand.

Dogs usually find it easier to comprehend hand signals compared to voice commands, primarily due to their inherent ability to read body language more effectively than understanding spoken words. In Stevie's case, however, given his inability to see, this approach was untenable. Despite this challenge, Stevie proved to be relatively easy to train as he could be lured into desired positions with food motivations, making the training process smoother.

The "stay" command did not receive excessive focus in Stevie's training. He learned to execute short stays, with the understanding that he was not permitted to move until I gave the release command. However, considering Stevie's high dependency on me, long stays with me not present were deemed too stressful for him.

In contrast, the "place" command was accorded high importance, as it involved Stevie being directed to his bed or a designated area where he was to stay until released. For Stevie, however, the implementation of this command involved slight modifications. Instead of sending him to his bed, I would escort him there, making sure it was strategically placed where he could hear me at all times.

If I happened to leave the area where Stevie was, I would assure him, "I am here; I am not leaving you." This was intended to provide him the assurance that I was nearby. To help reinforce this sense of security and familiarity, I consistently used the same dog bed or blanket. These items were designed to effectively convey the message to Stevie that I was always close by every time he was sent to stay on them. It was a process that involved significant time and repetition, but with diligence and patience, Stevie gradually grew more secure with staying on these items.

For training Stevie on recall, I implemented two specific commands: *here* and *come*. Each command carried its own distinct meaning and importance.

Firstly, the command, 'Come' was designed to signal Stevie to approach me at his own pace. It indicated that I needed him close, but it wasn't an urgent request. Generally, he would be rewarded with verbal praise or a gentle pat for obeying this command.

On the other hand, the command *here* indicated urgency. If Stevie heard me say *here*, he was expected to immediately cease whatever he was doing and rapidly return to me. Stevie was rewarded every single time he followed this command with something he highly valued. This command could prove crucial if he ever chased birds or was moving toward potential danger. By diligently rewarding Stevie each time he correctly responded to *here*, the importance and urgency of this command were underscored in his mind.

Stevie's training for the *here* command began with using a food lure. Guiding a treat in front of his nose, I would draw him toward me. As I simultaneously pronounced *here* and moved the treat from his nose to my knees, he was also lured into a sitting position. The moment he was seated, his behavior was marked with an affirmative and rewarded with a high-value treat. Stevie needed to comprehend that *here* meant more than just approaching me; it also required him to sit before me. The emphasis on sitting became important when on occasions, an excited Stevie would rush toward me, nudge me with his nose, and then swiftly dash off again!

Once Stevie began to understand the concept of the *here* command, I gradually stopped luring him toward me using food. Instead, I would call him and then clap my hands. The clapping sound established my location and helped him navigate toward me. I would always ensure the path between us was free of obstacles for his safe return.

Stevie quickly grasped the *here* command, and I was immensely proud of his progress. His keen ability to obediently respond to the command of *here* when called showcased his intelligence and his preparedness to react swiftly when necessary.

Stevie was always kept on a long line or leash for his safety during most of our outdoor adventures. However, he had an insatiable love for running off-leash, and I made it a point to afford him that liberty whenever it was safe to do so.

Observing Stevie relishing his moments of absolute freedom was indeed a heartwarming sight. Be it an open field or a sandy beach, the little brown dog would joyously bound across these expanses, epitomizing the sheer delight of unrestricted exploration. With his ears flapping in the breeze and his tail wagging incessantly, he radiated boundless happiness and liveliness.

Every so often, his keen nose would pick up a scent that intrigued him. This would invariably lead to abrupt halts in his lively run, followed by a frantic, keen-nosed search for the source of the intriguing scent. Upon locating the origin, he would sniff it with great interest and then, just as swiftly, resume his carefree dash across the expanse.

The sight of him running freely, basking in his world of exploration and discovery, was made possible not just by the safe environments but crucially by his mastery of the critical *here* command. His ability to respond promptly to this command was a testament to our training endeavors.

By complying consistently with the command and returning immediately to my side, Stevie was able to enjoy the luxury of off-leash outings. Thanks to his disciplined behavior and the training we worked through, Stevie could experience and express his natural instincts in a safe and joyful manner, just like every dog deserves to do.

Every morning, just as the sun painted the horizon with its first blush of pink and gold, I laced up my running shoes a ritual that marked the beginning of a new day and a particular time for Stevie and me. Knowing the importance of physical activity for Stevie's overall well-being and his alertness during the training sessions that lay ahead, I committed to a daily run. This routine quickly became the cornerstone of our day.

The soft rustling of the laces and the subtle squeak of the shoe's sole became an overture to adventure for Stevie. He seemed to have attuned himself to these auditory cues, the distinct sound, or perhaps the scent, of my running gear enough to trigger his eagerness. His tail would begin its merry wag, and in his excitement, he'd brush against my leg a clear sign of his readiness for the run.

Hannah, my loyal and spirited other dog, played a pivotal role in our outings, her presence providing Stevie with both companionship and guidance. As we set out, I would position Hannah between Stevie and me, a living buffer that instinctively understood her duty. With her there, Stevie could engage in our runs with vim and vigor but without the risk of surging ahead into uncertainty. Hannah was his compass, her steady pace and confident demeanor offering Stevie assurance and a model to emulate.

We carved out a route through the neighborhood that brought us through the awakening streets, where the chorus of the early morning birdsong and the whisper of leaves accompanied our synchronized strides. Hannah, ever vigilant, would lead with a deft awareness, setting a steady path while Stevie, securely in the middle, followed with a zealousness that was heartening to witness.

Remarkably, Stevie moved with a trust in his surroundings that could only come from the assurance of our presence and the predictable nature of our route. His strides were buoyant, his movements a testament to an indomitable spirit that refused to be caged by his lack of sight. Even as my feet pounded the pavement, sending reverberations up my shins, Stevie seemed to dance atop it, light and unencumbered.

The runs were more than exercise; they were a symphony of life in motion, an exemplar of adaptation and resilience. Stevie's wholehearted embrace of our daily routine, his reliance on the signals that told him it was time to don the invisible mantle of a runner, was nothing short of remarkable.

And so, with each daybreak, as I reached for my running shoes, the anticipation in Stevie's posture would grow, and I'd watch with a brimming pride as he readied himself to meet the dawn with the joy of a creature born to run.

The running in the mornings helped with his ability to walk in perfect harmony along my side when leashed. Utilizing the leash as a tangible line of communication between us, he would intently sense my movements a subtle urging forward, a minor deceleration, or a gentle shift in direction. The leash acted as our shared senses, guiding Stevie, creating a mental impression for him about his path, and informing him of when to modulate his pace.

Stevie was also highly perceptive of other minute indicators that helped him navigate. The rustling of my clothes, the consistent rhythm of my footsteps, and even the minute changes in my breathing pattern were all crucial sensory cues for him. Each of these nuances served as a signal, providing him with guidance throughout our shared journey.

His attuned instincts taught him that walking directly ahead could potentially result in bumps or bewilderment, prompting him to entrust his safety to my guidance. As such, instead of leading the way, he conscientiously walked beside me, responsive to my cues, with his movements reflecting shifts in mine.

With slight adjustments on the leash, I could convey whether we needed to turn right or left, get closer to me, or maintain more distance from my legs. The development of these leash cues was achieved through continual repetition and my consistent guidance. Initially, I guided him physically with the leash in the desired direction while concurrently verbalizing the commands *right* or *left*. Over time, Stevie learned to comprehend the meaning tied to each slight leash maneuver, and soon, a mere hint of movement was all it took for him to understand and respond accurately.

Leash manners laid the groundwork for environmental training, a crucial component of service dog training. This training was to help Stevie become familiar with and adapt to various scenarios and environments. The objective was to ensure that Stevie could operate satisfactorily in whichever situation we found ourselves, whether it was expected or unplanned.

Given Stevie's nature, certain environments raised specific concerns for me. Notably, environments where loud and unpredictable noises were prevalent such as crowded locales, concert venues, sports events, and silent places were potential challenges for Stevie. I was also cautious about places with strong odors, the presence of other animals, or food, given Stevie's heightened sense of smell and the potential for distractions.

To meet these challenges, Stevie needed wide-ranging exposure to numerous places, often repeatedly, to gradually desensitize him to these varying and sometimes unpredictable environmental factors. This slow, steady exposure aimed to foster his confidence, allowing him to remain balanced and well-behaved in any setting. Fortunately, Stevie's bold and fearless nature made this process relatively straightforward. Even though he occasionally got startled, his quick recovery time, paired with my reassuring presence, helped him regain composure swiftly.

Having two sons in school facilitated Stevie's exposure to an array of environments, as he was able to accompany me to their school events.

Both Sean, my older son, and Liam, the younger one, cherished Stevie's presence at their school. Sean was into wrestling, which meant attending loud and lively tournaments teeming with shouting and clapping audiences. These environments not only exposed Stevie to loud noises but also offered varied floor surfaces for him to walk and navigate.

On the other hand, Liam, who played the cello, provided a contrasting environment for Stevie. The musical performances exposed him to a distinctly different scenario awash with unique noises. Together, these diverse opportunities significantly contributed to Stevie's comprehensive environmental training, making him a more confident and adaptable service dog.

No matter where we ventured, be it bustling farmers' markets, tranquil parks, crowded events, or simple strolls around various busy neighborhoods, Stevie tackled every new environment with an endearing zeal and infectious enthusiasm. He seamlessly adapted to unfamiliar terrains, people, sounds, and scenarios with a fantastic spirit of resilience and adaptability.

I remember one particular afternoon, my dogs eagerly awaited our afternoon daily walk, as was the case every day. I thoroughly enjoyed those walks. Florida winters provided beautiful weather, tempting many neighbors to venture outside and embrace the pleasant atmosphere. It was an excellent opportunity to connect with the community, as some neighbors would often greet my dogs and engage in friendly conversations. This was another opportunity for Stevie to be out and about for more environmental exposure.

During the outing, as we sauntered along, I noticed Stevie beginning to slow his pace until he was practically crawling. This behavior change immediately caught my attention since Stevie had always embodied enthusiasm. Clearly, something was amiss that filled him with apprehension.

Curiosity piqued, I glanced around, searching for any potential source of fear that could explain Stevie's behavior. However, my eyes failed to detect anything out of the ordinary. Then, our neighbor, Linda, spotted us and expressed her concern, asking if everything was all right with Stevie. Linda had been a supportive neighbor for ages and was fond of Stevie, the neighborhood's joyous canine.

"I'm not sure, Linda, but it's evident something is making Stevie uncomfortable," I replied. Slowly making our way toward Linda, Stevie crawled at an even slower pace until he ultimately refused to move any farther, mere feet away from her.

At that moment, I realized why Stevie behaved the way he did. Something was off with Linda's health, and Stevie's instincts had picked up on it. I mustered the courage to ask Linda about her well-being, and to my surprise, she wore a look of astonishment as she questioned how I had come to know about her illness, particularly her battle with cancer. Linda had confided in no one about her condition.

With genuine concern, I revealed that it was the moment we approached her that Stevie's behavior shifted, tipping me off about the presence of an underlying medical issue. While I didn't know the exact nature of her ailment, I apologized and assured Linda that I was there for her should she require assistance.

Touched by the situation, Linda kneeled down and tenderly caressed

Stevie, comforting him while assuring us that she would be all right. It was a heartwarming sight, another testament to Stevie's extraordinary sensibility about changes.

As each day passed, Stevie grew more skilled and attuned to his role as my service dog. His unwavering dedication and understanding of my needs were transforming him into an irreplaceable companion.

Chapter 5

Becoming More

Stevie excelled in his service dog training program at only eight months old. He was showing advanced progress that was impressive for his young age. Alongside his service training, I noticed that Stevie also displayed qualities that could make him a good search-and-rescue (SAR) dog.

When I was deep in the throes of an intensive course geared toward becoming a certified professional police K9 trainer in North Carolina, an epiphany regarding Stevie's future career path dawned on me. Amidst these insightful classes, the seemingly adverse condition of Stevie's blindness was illuminated as a prospective strength. A vision began to take form in my mind: Stevie serving a noble purpose as a Human Remains Detection (HRD) dog is a pivotal asset within the ranks of search-and-rescue teams.

Yes, it is indeed the case that HRD dogs are integrated into SAR units. Such units routinely incorporate highly trained canines for an array of critical functions, including the location of missing individuals and the detection of human remains. Deploying dogs with specialized training in HRD is a significant boon across diverse SAR operations. Whether tasked amid the chaos underscored by natural disasters, the meticulous process that underscores criminal probes, or the unpredictable nature of expansive wilderness searches, these dogs' innate ability to detect and signal the presence of human remains proves indispensable. Their unique capacity fortifies the efforts of SAR personnel, enabling them to return lost individuals to their loved ones and procure vital evidence necessary for legal and forensic pursuits.

Convinced of Stevie's latent abilities and our profound bond, I thought he could distinguish himself in this highly specialized field. His exceptional senses compensation for his lack of sight coupled with his unshakable faith in my guidance provided a sturdy foundation for this path. Stevie's intrepidity further solidified my belief; his demeanor did not hint at trepidation, provided he was cognizant of my proximity.

Recognizing the potential for him to undergo search-and-rescue training, I wanted to ensure that this was a suitable path for him. Fortunately, during this time, I was friends with Janet, a certified master K9 trainer. I consulted with her to get a professional assessment of Stevie's capabilities.

A master dog trainer's recognition in the dog training community is by no means a small feat. The title is only bestowed upon individuals who have devoted countless years to the study of canine behavior, acquiring both empirical knowledge through hands-on experiences and theoretical understanding to comprehend the nuances of different dog temperaments and behaviors. Considering her professional acumen, Janet was the ideal person to approach for advice about steering Stevie's training toward a career in search-and-rescue operations.

With that aim in mind, I decided to reach out to Janet about my aspirations for Stevie. As soon as I began discussing Stevie's potential, Janet, ever the astute observer, could sense the excitement in my voice. However, she interjected with a dose of sobering reality before I could let my enthusiasm run wild.

"Marina," she cautioned, "as an experienced trainer, I can tell you that search-and-rescue dogs are versatile working dogs. They need to exhibit a particular blend of temperament and behavior traits to excel in their duties. I have a sneaking suspicion that Stevie might not possess these attributes. I'd need to evaluate him in person to give a more definite answer."

Janet had always been known for her frankness when discussing dogs' suitability for different roles, valuing honesty over sugarcoated reassurances. I deeply respected this trait, which is why I knew Janet would accurately appraise Stevie's capabilities.

With this aim, I prepared to make a trip to North Carolina to visit Janet for her expert assessment. Although flying was an option, I decided on a road trip instead, doubting whether Stevie was mentally prepared for his maiden flight. Thus, we embarked on a daunting twelve-hour-long drive. Fortunately, Stevie handled the journey remarkably well and enjoyed our frequent stops to stretch our legs and enjoy the scenery.

The day was beautifully bright and sunny when I rendezvoused with Janet at a park near her workplace. The park was an ideal venue, featuring a vast expanse of lush green grass punctuated by a few large obstacles, sufficiently big to prevent Stevie from bumping into them. These obstacles were noticeably large, like garbage bins, an ample tree, and a picnic table, well-spaced to facilitate Stevie's free movement.

Large, solid objects such as trees and big containers often disrupt the airflow around them, creating a unique air pattern. For Stevie, his sensitive whiskers, or vibrissae, adeptly pick up these subtle alterations in air currents, signaling him about the presence of a potential obstacle in his path. Additionally, these whiskers can detect even the gentlest vibrations, which could further hint at an encroaching hazard or impediment.

Stevie could likely differentiate between the specific odors that various objects emit. In this context, a garbage container embodies a myriad of scents, a fact rather unpleasant to us but beneficial for a canine partner like Stevie.

The smells radiating from the garbage could serve as a unique identifier for him, indicating the container's presence in his immediate surroundings. Even more fascinating is those different materials be they plastic, metal, or wood give off distinct smells, potentially helping Stevie distinguish between different types of obstacles.

The picnic area was specifically tranquil, as it was restricted by a concrete surface a distinct contrast to the soft grass, which made it easier for Stevie to differentiate between the terrains and maneuver accordingly, thereby avoiding a collision with the table and benches. The park perimeter opened up to a quaint little creek accessible by a small step. Even if Stevie strayed toward the creek due to the uncontainable excitement he usually exhibited while sprinting around grassy knolls, the small height of the step ensured that he wouldn't get injured.

A whirlwind of excitement and anxious anticipation enveloped me. I was well acquainted with Stevie's potential, but it was Janet's opinion that I earnestly yearned for before commencing any intensive rescue training.

Seeing Janet after an extended period filled me with warmth. After our pleasant greetings, she seemed eager to meet my affectionate pooch, Stevie. We proceeded toward the car, where Stevie waited in his crate. With a fond glance at Stevie, Janet admired his endearing brown coat and gorgeous eyes. Bursting with pride, I told her, "Janet, you'll be amazed to see him run around freely, oblivious to his blindness!"

Once I had guided Stevie out of the car, we ventured toward a suitable area to let him off the leash. Before doing so, Janet wanted to assess his sociability and confidence around strangers fundamental traits for effective search-and-rescue dogs. She knelt and called Stevie's name. I knew Stevie had a curious but cautious approach toward strangers, typically identifying their presence by sniffing the air and turning his head toward them. However, he prioritized their attention only upon identifying a calm aura around them through their scent and my behavior.

Stevie instantly turned his head toward Janet at the sound of his name. He got up, wagged his tail enthusiastically, and moved toward Janet. He sniffed her and attempted to lick her face in a friendly gesture. Janet's amusement was palpable as she laughed and stated, "What a sweet boy he is; it's evident that he's passed the socialization assessment with absolutely flying colors."

The moment had arrived for Stevie to be set free. I always ensured that he sat quietly before unfastening his leash, asking him excitedly, "Are you ready?" As his ears perked up in anticipation, I cheerfully declared, "Go, Stevie, you are free." The sound of *go* was all he needed, and like clockwork, he sprang to his feet and bolted off, his euphoria mirroring that of a tornado in full swing.

Janet could only voice her astonishment, stating, "Wow, what a confident little dog! Running this way without knowing where he is going." We stood back and watched Stevie dart around the sizable park, fearlessly exploring his surroundings. It was a testament to his joy and boundless energy. Janet noted that Stevie didn't fear straying too far from me. Every now and then, he would gambol back to my side briefly, seemingly verifying my presence, and then set off to explore once again with unmatched zest.

Gradually, our curiosity shifted toward determining his high drive an innate instinct in dogs causing them to engage vigorously in a particular activity. Typically, dogs with high drive exhibit unyielding focus and determination when it comes to executing specific tasks. This could range from chasing a ball to herding livestock or tracking and tracing scents. We aimed to gauge whether Stevie possessed this trait by observing his reaction to pursuing a ball and tracking its scent when hidden. We did not need to hide the toy as is done with sighted dogs because Stevie never sees where the ball is.

To begin the test, I positioned Stevie beside me, gripping his collar firmly to keep him steady. As soon as he heard the squeak of his favorite red ball, Stevie knew it was time to play fetch. After I tossed the ball not too far away, causing it to bounce a couple of times before halting, Stevie instantly recognized its sound. As I released him, he darted straight toward the location of the sound. However, he overshot it initially, only to abruptly halt, sniff the ground, and backtrack to the ball's location. He was approximately ten feet off initially, but his innate sense of direction soon kicked in, guiding him straight to the ball. Like a beacon guiding him back, Stevie quickly found his way to where I had been standing, the ball firmly grasped in his mouth. His navigational accuracy was truly impressive.

Eager to see his reaction when the ball was placed without him hearing its landing, Janet placed it around thirty feet away in the opposite direction. I grinned at her suggestion, confident in Stevie's abilities.

Now in full fetch mode, all it took for Stevie to launch his search was for the collar to be released. Initially, he headed in the direction where he'd found the ball last, investigating that spot for a moment before plunging into his quest again. His search strategy was methodical, starting before us as he traced a zigzag course with his nose to the ground. He alternated his approach by circling the area, starting wide and gradually narrowing until suddenly, he lunged into the air as if startled by something beneath him. Sure enough, he had stumbled upon his toy yet again!

Janet wanted Stevie to trace the ball's path from the start for the final test. She rolled the ball on the ground so Stevie could pick up the trail from where it began. Precariously, Stevie positioned his snout close to the ground, beginning his quest to trace the invisible scent trail left by the ball. Even as he followed the trail, he instinctively zigzagged across it, retracing his path frequently to focus only on the strongest source of scent. His movements were smooth and calculated, demonstrating his unwavering determination to complete his task.

Janet was delighted, acknowledging Stevie's talent. "Wow, Stevie, you really are something else!" She enthusiastically extolled, "He clearly displays a high drive and uses his scent-tracking capabilities to locate his toy, regardless of obstacles. He even tries different strategies until he finds the one that leads him to success. Well done, little one. It's time to have some rest."

As Stevie enjoyed a little respite, Janet and I discussed his capabilities. She admired Stevie's confidence and acknowledged he had the essential qualifications to develop into an excellent working dog. However, she clarified that this wouldn't necessarily guarantee his suitability for the search-and-rescue line of work. Given his visual impairment, it would largely depend on the effectiveness of my training skills and how well Stevie could adapt.

Concerns emerged regarding his ability to navigate challenging terrains riddled with deep slopes, uneven rocks, and the entangled roots of robust trees. The prospect of Stevie traversing through spring waters, plummeting downslope along mountain walls, or maneuvering through other strenuous landscapes even those that presented difficulty for sighted dogs seemed daunting.

Yet, I harbored profound faith in both Stevie's capabilities and my training competence. I was determined to train Stevie and transition him into a search-and-rescue K9. Janet was confident in my ability and believed we were well-equipped to succeed.

As we pondered the most suitable discipline for Stevie, Janet let her dog out to frolic with Stevie, providing a playful distraction to our serious deliberations.

Janet explained that each discipline within search and rescue required distinct training and unique skill sets. She suggested we consider air scenting, which involves non-scent-specific searching for human odors. Typically conducted off-leash, these dogs explore expansive wilderness areas, often moving off the beaten paths, while their handlers remain on more straightforward, human-accessible terrain.

One significant concern regarding Stevie's potential role as an air-scenting dog was that such tasks are typically performed off-leash. This mode of operation means that Stevie would have to navigate search areas without the direct physical guidance of a leash, which could lead to moments when I lose direct visual contact with him. Given Stevie's blindness, this posed a substantial risk. The absence of a visual link between us could render me unable to ensure his safety effectively, leaving him vulnerable to the inherent dangers of uncertain terrains or hazardous environments he might encounter. Such risks could range from minor injuries to more severe life-threatening situations, which was a risk I was not willing to take lightly.

Something caught my eye as I sat engrossed in Janet's lively chatter. At the periphery of my vision, I noticed the sudden absence of Stevie. He had been playfully trotting behind Janet's dog along the tranquil creek his tiny paws creating a rhythmic pattern on the damp mud. Janet's dog had momentarily paused to investigate a scent by the creek's edge. Amid his explorative venture, Stevie continued to trot, his focus unwavering from their path.

His movement toward the creek was a spectacle of unwavering determination; however, his attention to his surroundings was quite the opposite. Unmindful of the impending little step or edge, Stevie, in his obliviousness, tripped over and plummeted into the creek. I scrambled to my feet and rushed over to him, only to witness a scene akin to tranquility. He was drinking water from the creek with a placid serenity. He managed to find the water without panicking!

I could only imagine that the captivating sound of the gently flowing water, its refreshing aroma, along the unique sweetness in its taste might have piqued Stevie's curiosity. The earthy fragrance of moist soil and mud interlacing with the dewy freshness of the water must have attracted him. Once satiated, he effortlessly spun around, only to stun me as he made an unexpected high jump back onto the edge of the creek.

"Oh, what a clever boy you are, Stevie," I commended as my heart swelled with pride. He turned his head toward the direction of my voice although not quite looking at me his head slightly tilted in endearing curiosity for a fleeting second before he descended back to the creek.

Observing our interaction, Janet chuckled and commented, "I can see how much fun you have with him. He truly is an energetic ball of fur."

I agreed with a contented smile, "Indeed, he is relentless, which keeps me on my toes, but I wouldn't have it any other way."

While observing Stevie investigating around the creek, we continued with our conversation.

Exploring alternative avenues, we considered the specialization of trailing or tracking work for Stevie. These disciplines involve a dog homing in on the distinct scent of a particular individual, following their path with precision. Trailing and tracking usually necessitate that the dog remains on a leash, which provides the handler with control and ensures the dog's safety as it works. This aspect made these areas of expertise seem much more suitable for Stevie.

Operating with the security of a leash would mitigate the risks associated with off-leash searches and would allow me to protect and guide Stevie as he harnessed his heightened sense of smell. By focusing on the unique scent of a specific person, Stevie could be trained to carefully follow their trail, all while safely tethered to my side. This controlled approach could allow Stevie to excel as a working dog in a capacity that accommodates his lack of sight while prioritizing his well-being.

Urban Disaster Search was another area of specialty. These dogs are critical in locating survivors trapped under debris in urban settings following disasters. While acknowledging the critical role these dogs play under the Federal Emergency Management Agency (FEMA) an organization responsible for responding to and mitigating major crises in the United States it became evident that the rigorous FEMA criteria for training such dogs would exceed Stevie's and my capacities.

Janet ultimately suggested that we consider training Stevie as a Human Remains Detection (HRD) dog, aligning perfectly with my envisioned role. One significant benefit of this specialty was its adaptability in terms of training locations. Unlike other K9 working disciplines, where an array of volunteers is necessary to pose as "subjects" for the canines to locate, HRD training is markedly less dependent on human participation. It can be conducted in various settings without requiring multiple people to be present, offering a level of independence in how and where training sessions can take place.

Additionally, the type of training involved in preparing a dog for HRD work is inherently diverse and intriguing. It's designed to engage a dog's innate abilities, challenging them with a range of tasks that are meant to be both mentally stimulating and physically demanding. For Stevie, this would serve as a robust training regimen to hone his skills and as a constructive outlet for his energy. The array of scenarios presented in HRD training would keep him alert, focused, and eager to work, offering him an array of sensory experiences to investigate and overcome.

This aspect of HRD training was particularly advantageous for Stevie, as the stimulating and varied nature of the exercises would rival the typical routine disruption caused by his blindness. It would instead draw upon his strengths, providing him with a fulfilling and engaging occupation that would take full advantage of his remarkable scent capabilities and offer him plenty of mental and physical enrichment.

Reflecting on my initial instincts about Stevie's potential as a Human Remains Detection (HRD) dog, I felt a profound sense of validation when Janet echoed my sentiments. Her professional opinion reinforced my belief that pursuing this path could harness Stevie's unique skills and turn them into an asset for HRD work.

As we embarked on the journey back to Florida, my mind meticulously mapped out a training strategy tailored to Stevie's needs and abilities. I contemplated a structured training regimen that would methodically harness Stevie's keen sense of smell and adapt it to the specialized demands of HRD tasks. I aimed to develop a step-by-step program that would gradually introduce Stevie to the rigors of HRD work, nurturing his natural talents and guiding him toward mastery of the discipline.

Considering Stevie's blindness, I recognized the need for a careful and considerate approach to his training. I envisioned a series of incremental challenges that would cater to his sensory strengths and ensure his comfort and safety. I thought about the types of environments where we could train, the kinds of scent sources we might use, and the cues and commands that would most effectively guide him.

My plans became increasingly refined throughout the drive, taking shape as a comprehensive blueprint for Stevie's future development. My goal was to make the process an enjoyable and rewarding experience for Stevie, transforming him into a proficient HRD dog who could confidently and effectively carry out his duties.

Chapter 6

Search And Rescue Training

Once back in Florida, the stage was set to commence the Human Remains Detection (HRD) training program for Stevie. This specialized training venture was designed to capitalize on his unique sensory capabilities and adapt them for a vital role in search-and-rescue operations. The plan involved a series of targeted exercises and progressive learning steps, each aimed at equipping Stevie with the necessary skills to locate and indicate human remains based on scent detection. With meticulous planning and a commitment to Stevie's growth as an HRD dog, we were ready to undertake this new and vital chapter in his training journey.

Stevie's blindness introduced unique challenges that demanded an innovative approach to traditional human remains detection training. Training dogs for scent detection is an organized and sequential approach that equips dogs with the skills to identify and communicate the detection of specific odors. This training regimen entails a series of steps, beginning with introducing the target scent and gradually conditioning the dog to respond to that scent in a distinguishable manner. The goal is for the dog to alert its handler reliably and accurately when it has discovered the scent it has been trained to detect. This is often achieved through positive reinforcement techniques, where the dog is rewarded for successful identification, thereby reinforcing the desired behavior of indicating the presence of the particular scent.

Training Stevie for the intricate task of odor detection required access to olfactory elements that were authentic to human beings. Artificially manufactured scents simply wouldn't suffice for the high level of precision needed. Our training materials would be sourced from authentic human biological samples, including blood, nails, teeth, and hair, and, eventually, would extend to encompass bones.

Perhaps you're curious about the collection process for these remarkably specific scent items. The journey to acquire each was as unique as the items themselves:

For blood procurement, necessity birthed an elegantly simple solution I used my own. Indeed, the uncertainty of personal connections played a fortuitous role; an acquaintance of mine worked as an emergency room doctor. He would draw a sample of my blood precisely governed by professional expertise. This crimson vital fluid was carefully allocated into an array of containers, each containing a different volume. Such variance allowed us to create gradients of odor intensity, a crucial factor for meticulous scent training.

Also, for the collection of blood samples, I was fortunate enough to have a supportive network of friends who understood the importance of our work. These friends were well-acquainted with my passion and Stevie's unique training goals.

Whenever their child had a minor mishap, like a nosebleed or a scraped knee, which inevitably led to blood stains on their clothes, they thought of us. Instead of tossing the clothing into the laundry, they carefully set it aside. They knew that even such ordinary incidents could provide invaluable training materials for Stevie.

Once the stained clothes were in my possession, Stevie and I would use them for his training exercises. After each training session, I took great care to wash these items thoroughly, erasing all traces of blood. Once clean and dry, I folded them neatly and prepared them for return. Alongside the clothing, I included a heartfelt thank you note, expressing my gratitude for their contribution to Stevie's development. It was a small gesture to acknowledge their part in equipping Stevie with the skills to help others potentially. Each piece of clothing, now clean and folded, carried stories of growth and scraped knees transformed into a legacy of service.

As for teeth, an item one might assume challenging to source, the endeavor was surprisingly straightforward. My dentist showcased a benevolent spirit and a curiosity piqued by the mission. He provided decayed teeth that had been slated for disposal some even bearing minuscule remnants of tissue.

The gathering of nails was a more protracted affair, dependent on the collective patience and contributions of those in my intimate circle. It involved salvaging the typically discarded slivers from routine nail trimming, compiling small troves over time. My children, my husband, and a cadre of friends generously participated, all sharing in the gathered harvest meant for Stevie's training.

Hair, in comparison to the other materials, was a bounty bestowed with ease. Following a typical session with the hairstylists, I seized the opportunity and explain my request for the trimmings that would, under ordinary circumstances, be swept into obscurity. The stylist, moved by the grander purpose, handed over the clippings with enthusiasm and pride her everyday work now linked to the grander tapestry of service through Stevie's forthcoming achievements.

It was a collection process that hinged on community and the intricate web of support surrounding a military-bound service and search dog like Stevie. Each donor, knowingly or unknowingly, played their part in weaving the invisible net of Stevie's future successes.

Securing bones, which are fundamental for the advanced segment of Stevie's scent detection training, might appear perplexing. However, obtaining them was far less complicated than one might imagine. A niche market exists companies that specialize in providing genuine human bones, primarily catering to the educational sector. Occasionally, these bones are damaged or possess imperfections, rendering them unsuitable for medical study or academic purposes. Such imperfections, however, have no bearing on their utility for scent training they retain the distinct organic scent profile we require.

For our purposes, thankfully, we didn't need an entire skeleton. A small quantity of human bone was sufficient to imprint the scent for Stevie's olfactory training. Focusing on efficiency and necessity, I acquired what is commonly referred to as a SAR (Search and Rescue) Training bone package.

This carefully curated set included an assortment of bones typically found in both the hand and foot, along with a single vertebra. With these genuine specimens in hand, we were well-equipped to proceed with the crucial task of familiarizing Stevie with the scent of human bones, setting the stage for his development into a proficient search-and-rescue dog.

Generally, for search-and-rescue dogs, toys are chosen as rewards instead of food. Toys can often keep a dog mentally stimulated for longer durations. For instance, once a dog is rewarded with a toy, playtime can continue, which makes the reward last longer. When dogs are rewarded with a toy, the result is often a play session between the handler and the dog. While this is great for bonding and utilizing a dog's prey drive, the energetic play can mean sessions must be limited to prevent the dog from becoming overly tired or winded.

Conversely, you can perform more repetitions and prolonged training sessions when using food. This is because once the reward (i.e., food) is given, it's consumed quickly, and the training can continue with the dog's attention refocused on the next command.

In the end, both reward methods come with their own advantages and disadvantages. What to use depends largely on the dog's preferences and the training circumstances. The choice between food and toys for training rewards depends on the dog's drive and what kind of training is being done. Stevie loved both!

During the various stages of service training, I used treats extensively as positive reinforcers in our service dog sessions. So, I decided to reserve toys for his search-and-rescue training, creating a distinct separation between the two disciplines. Fortunately, Stevie was an enthusiastic pup with a broad love for all kinds of toys, whether soft plushies, hard rubber balls, squeaky playthings, or the occasional unexpected item.

Stevie had a particularly mischievous habit: he was an expert at sniffing out and stealthily procuring my son's toys, his nose guiding him to the jackpot every time. If there was a ball or stuffed animal within his reach, you could bet Stevie would find it. His playful thefts were endearing, though not always without consequence. And then there were the socks, Stevie's forbidden treasures. Like many of his canine counterparts, he couldn't resist the allure of worn, fragrant socks. It was a love affair with my boys' laundry the dirtier, the better for our Stevie.

Despite his fondness for socks, Stevie was lucky, or perhaps *resilient* might be the better word. Thankfully, each sock he surreptitiously swallowed was regurgitated before it could cause any real harm. Yet, it still was a cause for concern.

One such memorable incident unfolded when Stevie and I were away on a three-week intensive training trip in North Carolina. One quiet morning, as the first light of dawn crept through the windows, I was greeted not by the face of my loyal companion but by the less pleasant sight of vomit. After ensuring Stevie was his usual lively self, unaffected by whatever had upset his stomach, I turned my attention to the mess he'd left behind. Amid the pile, I spotted the unmistakable icon of a Mickey Mouse sock a surprising revelation considering we'd been away from home for over two weeks, revealing the sock's lengthy and unwanted residency in Stevie's stomach.

This incident underscored a serious talk I needed to have with Sean and Liam, my boys. Returning home, we gathered for a family meeting where I explained the dangers of Stevie's sock-eating habit how it wasn't just a quirky behavior but a potential health risk that could lead to a dire need for surgery. The boys listened intently, their young minds grasping the gravity of the situation. They earnestly pledged to keep their socks out of Stevie's reach, stowing them safely in the laundry basket.

I couldn't help but wonder about the success of our new household protocol. Whether it was the diligence of Sean and Liam or Stevie's own decision to swear off socks, I can't say. But from then on, not a single sock went missing, and Stevie had no more unscheduled vomiting sessions. Perhaps it was a bit of both the boys becoming more responsible and Stevie losing his "acquired" taste for such a snack.

Whatever the case, I was grateful for the outcome, and Stevie continued to thrive in his training, sock-free and ready to serve.

Given his boundless enthusiasm for playthings, toys were selected as the ideal reward for Stevie. Yet, the real challenge lay not in his fondness for toys but in his capacity to distinguish the complex odors linked with each toy during our training sessions focused on scent detection.

With a collection of required scents, the next step was the odor introduction phase. Stevie needed to become acquainted with the specific scent he was being trained to identify, a scent often concealed within an item the toys, in his case. I selected a specially designed ball peppered with holes for this endeavor. Carefully, I placed small amounts of the scent samples, each securely locked within its own Ziplock bag to avoid any intermingling of odors. This practice is similar to the methods used in training dogs for narcotics or explosives detection, but rest assured, no dangerous substances are ever employed in our exercises. Today, we often utilize substitute scents designed to mimic the real ones, assuring the safety and well-being of the dogs during their training.

The ball I chose for Stevie had all the odors he needed to commit to memory. Having all the odors in the same toy, I took advantage of a dog's remarkable talent for olfactory differentiation. Unlike humans, who might simply detect the collective aroma of a freshly baked cake, unable to pinpoint the individual scents of its components, dogs have a far superior sense of smell. They can discern each unique ingredient vanilla, flour, eggs, sugar, and butter distinctly, even when these elements have been combined and transformed through baking. This incredible ability is precisely why, as Stevie advanced in his training and the odors were eventually separated, he would have the capacity to identify each one on its own.

By using the ball, Stevie created a positive association with the target odors. Then, it was time to play fetch! Every time Stevie retrieved the toy, it unwittingly interacted with the odor concealed within it. With sighted dogs, the game gradually intensifies to engage their olfactory senses and make them rely less on their vision. With Stevie, that was not the case. What I did with Stevie instead was to place the ball in places where to get it, he had to go over obstacles, like boxes and luggage, making the fetch game a little more challenging for him. I also started placing the ball inside the boxes and luggage pieces.

Stevie had mastered the skill of fetching scent ball flawlessly. During this period, we only play fetch with that ball to train him to recognize the target odor as the only scent that will lead to a reward, the scent ball, the toy.

Even though Stevie was doing great with the fetch game, an issue arose when I was introducing the next training phase.

In this level, I aim to train Stevie to identify the odor independently, without the scent-concealing toy as a guide. This training level aims to teach dogs to recognize specific smells without relying on the toy as a cue. To achieve this, individual odors are presented using boxes. Each box is a small cube measuring one inch in length, width, and height, with a hole at the top large enough for the dog to introduce its nose. The box is placed on the ground. Dogs possess a natural curiosity, and when they encounter something new in their environment, they instinctively approach and investigate it. The purpose of using boxes in training is to contain the scent within them. The scent is trapped inside the box, with the only means of escape being a small hole located on the top. This hole is designed specifically for the dog to introduce its nose and investigate the scent further.

When the dog places its nose in the hole of the box, it is rewarded with his toy. With sight dogs, the toy is thrown to the dog by the box. This reward serves as positive reinforcement for correctly engaging with the odor. Gradually, the dog is trained to associate a particular behavior with the presence of the odor inside the box. Common behavioral indications include sitting, lying down, pawing at the box, or a frozen stare.

Once the dog becomes proficient at indicating the presence of the odor with a single box, additional boxes are introduced to develop the dog's searching abilities. Through this training method, dogs will learn to generalize the scent recognition behavior and apply it to different boxes, enabling them to effectively search for specific odors.

To modify the training approach for Stevie, I deliberately chose to change the method of placing the odor. Instead of using boxes, I decided to utilize a brick. Stevie's visual impairment influenced this decision, as he could not recognize or navigate around the boxes visually. Furthermore, using boxes would only add another challenge for Stevie during the search process.

I effectively removed this extra obstacle by placing the odor underneath a brick. The brick served the dual purpose of securely holding the odor sample in place while providing a more accessible target for Stevie.

Given Stevie's tendency to begin his search with his nose near the ground, I believed this alternative approach would be more conducive to his natural search behavior. It allowed him to concentrate solely on detecting and locating the odor without any needless hindrances or unnecessary barriers impeding his progress.

The initial trial with Stevie went well as he successfully detected the cadaver odor under the brick and was rewarded with his toy. This initial success filled me with excitement and optimism. However, subsequent attempts with Stevie did not go as planned.

Instead of searching for the cadaver odor, Stevie became fixated on searching for his toy during our training sessions. Despite my repeated attempts, Stevie seemed to misunderstand the objective of the training, focusing on retrieving or finding his toy rather than detecting the scent.

Perplexed and slightly frustrated by this unexpected behavior, I sought advice and guidance from Janet. Instead of suggesting conventional methods, Janet encouraged me to think outside the box and be creative in designing a training approach that would effectively teach Stevie to detect the cadaver odor while overcoming his fixation on the toy. Janet's belief in my ability to find a solution and her positive attitude gave me the motivation and inspiration to continue working toward a successful training strategy for Stevie.

"Stevie, it's important for me to find a method to effectively communicate what I want you to learn. Let's take a short break from our training sessions so that I can find a better way to help you understand. I believe that with patience and perseverance, we will achieve our goals together. Reflecting on my conversation with Janet, I realized that part of the challenge may have been my approach. It seemed that I had been trying to progress too quickly in our training without allowing for proper comprehension and success on your part." As I spoke these words to Stevie, he attentively faced me, seemingly unable to comprehend the specifics of what I was saying but undeniably animated by the sound of my voice.

While determining the best approach for Stevie's training, I decided to focus on another crucial aspect of search-and-rescue training.

Search-and-rescue dogs must be trained to familiarize themselves with different environments like service dogs. However, the environments that search-and-rescue dogs may work in can be much more varied, unpredictable, and challenging than those that service dogs typically encounter.

I focused on three key environmental areas: rural, water, and wilderness. Since urban environments were already covered in Stevie's service dog training, I directed my attention toward other settings. A unique advantage we had was that Stevie excelled in night and low-light conditions to him, it was no different from his natural habitat!

When introducing Stevie to these new environments, it was evident that he thoroughly enjoyed every moment. For him, it was like playtime and an opportunity to revel in the joys of life. However, out of all the environments, Stevie had a particular affinity for water areas. Whether it was the beach, lakes, creeks, or swamps, Stevie displayed immense enthusiasm, and I knew these environments would pose no difficulties for him due to his deep love for water.

The water areas provided Stevie with a sense of familiarity and comfort, allowing him to excel in his search-and-rescue training. His natural passion for water made these training sessions even more enjoyable and effective.

Stevie became my loyal sidekick, accompanying me everywhere, and each new place presented itself to Stevie like an open classroom. The world was teeming with ample opportunities for him to learn, grow, and amass an expansive vocabulary. Our communication became far-reaching and complex through persistent repetition and my constant verbal cues.

The wildness was going to be the most challenging environment for Stevie. That's why I took it upon myself to introduce Stevie to many physical elements in his immediate surroundings, such as steps, hills, jumps, pools, and stairs. For instance, I would verbally state "stairs" to signal the upcoming ascent while approaching the stairs. As we began to climb, I would say "step" to correspond with each elevation change. Once we reached the top, I would announce "done." Over time, Stevie learned to associate my command of "stairs" with the act of climbing steps, continuing until he heard the word "done," and I no longer needed to say "step." I would use the cue "step" for only a few steps in a row. He even knew that if I said, "big step," it meant it was taller than average. Occasionally, if I became distracted and neglected to say "done" after climbing steps, Stevie would amusingly continue to walk as if he were still climbing stairs.

In teaching Stevie a rich descriptive palette of words, I handed him a toolbox that he would need to navigate his world more confidently and effectively. These words became valuable cues, unlocking Stevie's ability to perceive and understand his surroundings in greater depth, thereby helping him evolve into the resourceful SAR dog I aspired for him to be. I could not help but appreciate Stevie's patience and tolerance, even as he brought a smile to my face with his comedic high steps when I forgot to say "done."

Stevie was truly excelling in his training, but I must admit that there were times when my mistakes hindered our progress. Even now, I have a bittersweet memory etched in my heart of a particular incident involving Stevie and my vehicle.

That day was just like any other, with the familiar routines guiding our actions like the invisible threads of habit. Stevie, always wise beyond the norm, had grown accustomed to the symphony of our daily activities. With each new lesson, his repertoire of recognized sounds expanded, and so did his confidence. He had learned the clinking metal the hushed thud of the back door to my SUV swinging open sounds that heralded an imminent journey.

I looped my purse over my shoulder, keys jangling softly as Stevie padded beside me, a soft silhouette of anticipation. He moved with purpose, each step a testament to his trust in the world I helped him navigate. As we neared the vehicle, I reached for the handle, my fingers grazing the cool metal, the back door beginning its yawning arc open.

But in that precise sliver of time, distraction came calling in the form of my neighbor's voice. A friendly hello, a query about the upcoming weekend, something simple yet effectively jolting: my attention, momentarily captured, left the door only partially ajar. The familiar sound, however, had already unfurled into the space between us like an invisible command.

There was no time to react. The sound of impact a hollow crash that cut through the morning calm had my heart plummeting. I whipped around, fearing the worst.

"Oh no!" The words tore from me two syllables heavy with worry. Ever the keen and responsive student, Stevie had leaped at the half-open door, expecting the welcoming gap that was always there. But this time, the steady, reliable world we had curated together betrayed him.

My sweet boy had collided with the unyielding surface of the car's back door. Guilt washed over me like an unwelcome tide. How crucial my role was in shaping his reality, and how fragile that reality could be. I approached him quickly, words tumbling over each other in a flurry of concern.

"Stevie, my sweet boy, are you okay? I am so sorry for not being more careful." My hands, steady trainers now transformed into comfort instruments, skimmed over him checking, assuring, soothing. Every stroke of my hand was a silent apology, an unspoken promise to guard him more fiercely.

And yet, in true Stevie fashion, the grace he carried in his soul shone through the mishap. His tail continued its unfettered rhythm, embodying forgiving natures and unclouded joy. His wet nose found my cheek, and gentle kisses reassured me more than words ever could. "What an amazing little dog you are, Stevie. Thanks for forgiving me while I was not paying attention to you."

At that moment, my respect for Stevie deepened. Not just for the exceptional dog he was but for the spirit he encapsulated one of resilience, trust, and an unwavering ability to find the light, even when the door seemed closed.

Stevie, my extraordinary blind boy, was undergoing training to fulfill the demanding roles of both a service dog and a search-and-rescue dog. As I looked into Stevie's endearing face, I couldn't help but wonder if it was too overwhelming for him. With a tender tone, I murmured, "Am I asking too much of my sweet boy by training you for these dual responsibilities?"

Despite my concerns, Stevie's unwavering attitude and body language spoke volumes. He seemed to revel in every training session, his enthusiasm radiating through his entire being. Never once did he indicate that the training was too much for him. It was I, viewing the situation through the lens of a human, who entertained doubts about the intensity of his training.

However, Stevie's perspective was vastly different. Each day was a new opportunity for him to embark on thrilling adventures, and he embarked on them with me by his side. His sheer joy and zest for life were evident in every wag of his tail and sparkle in his eyes. Stevie's unwavering happiness served as a gentle reminder that he adored every aspect of his training nothing was too great a challenge for him.

In the end, it was my own worries and concerns that overshadowed the astonishing resilience and enthusiasm that Stevie demonstrated every day. His love for life and unyielding spirit showed me that he could handle anything that came his way, including the formidable task of training for two vital roles simultaneously.

However, crafting a training regimen for Stevie required a discerning approach because of his dual role. As a service dog, he needed to learn to identify the early indicators of my migraines, while his training as a search-and-rescue dog focused on detecting human remains. To avoid any confusion between these two very different responsibilities, it was imperative to separate these training sessions in his routine clearly. My goal was to ensure that Stevie could effortlessly switch between his roles, understanding the distinct expectations and tasks that came with each context.

First, I opted to use different equipment for each training type. Stevie was equipped with a distinct service dog harness for his service dog training more akin to a vest. This vest served a dual purpose: it alerted people to Stevie's status as a service animal, requesting them not to pet him, thereby avoiding distractions; additionally, it accommodated my medication. For these sessions, I relied on a martingale collar, one of my favorites for dog training to accentuate the difference. A martingale collar features a larger part that encircles the dog's neck and a smaller section where the leash gets attached. Its unique aspect lies in its design should the dog attempt to escape, the collar automatically tightens due to the leash's pull, securing the dog without causing discomfort.

In sharp contrast, for the SAR training, Stevie was fitted with a harness designed explicitly for heavy-pulling tasks, and I removed the martingale collar. When on his SAR duties, navigating cadaver detection terrains, I mainly followed him, acting as a handler. My primary role was to ensure his safety and assist him in accessing any difficult spots he wished to explore. The way Stevie carried himself when in his SAR attire radiated a sense of determination and pride. He was visibly aware of the task and that the responsibility of leading the search lay on his shoulders. Though our search activities often seemed unstructured (but not in Stevie's mind), with sporadic direction changes and a frenetic pace, I trusted his instincts. Despite the appearance of seeming confusion, I knew Stevie had the nuanced technique that he was working with.

Cleverly contrasting the two sessions was their pace and setting. Stevie's service dog training was often slow-paced and quiet, typically conducted indoors, allowing for a calm and controlled environment. Conversely, cadaver detection training involved high-energy sessions filled with active movement, all set in the exciting ambiance of the great outdoors. This stark difference in training conditions played an integral role in helping Stevie distinguish between the two types of sessions.

After realizing that toys were not effective for Stevie to associate with the odor, I decided to use food as a training tool instead. Unlike working dogs, who are rewarded by having the toy thrown at them when they find the odor, I couldn't do the same with Stevie and food due to the mess and confusion it would create. Therefore, I used a clicker as a marker to indicate when Stevie found the odor, which was later replaced by a verbal cue of "yes." Stevie would associate the clicker sound with the food reward when using a clicker as a training tool. Dolphin training methods inspire this use of markers. In dolphin training, trainers blow a whistle to let the dolphins know they did a good job and will receive a food reward. Similarly, with Stevie, I used the clicker as a marker to signal that he successfully located the odor and completed his job. I didn't mark the behavior until I was close by, placing my hand in front of his nose to promptly provide the reward.

You might wonder why I initially used a clicker as a marker before switching to a verbal cue. Firstly, timing is crucial in dog training. The clicker's distinct and consistent sound helps to precisely mark the desired behavior without any variations in tone or volume. Its sharp and quick sound enables accurate timing, essential for dogs with shorter attention spans and faster learning capacities. In contrast, verbal cues can be variable, leading to confusion for the dog in understanding which behavior is being rewarded.

Using food as a reward instead of a toy proved highly effective with Stevie. He quickly learned that when he successfully located the human remains odors, he would be rewarded with a delectable piece of chicken or steak. I made sure to use a very high-value reward during training, as Stevie was highly motivated to earn that delicious piece of meat.

Stevie's understanding of indicating the presence of the odor developed rapidly. I allowed Stevie to choose his own indication, as it is important for the dog to feel comfortable with their chosen behavior. In Stevie's case, he naturally opted to lie down and freeze as his indication. I believe this behavior was influenced by the odor being placed underneath a brick on the ground. Once Stevie learned that he had to lie down and freeze after locating the odor beneath the brick, I instructed him to pinpoint the exact location.

Teaching Stevie to pinpoint the exact location was surprisingly easy. After Stevie had successfully indicated the presence of the odor by lying down and freezing, I would instruct him to "show me." Although he didn't comprehend my words, communicating with him this way triggered a thought process. He began to consider the possibility that the odor might not be there anymore, prompting him to check the area again to confirm its presence. Once he was certain that the odor was still there, he would lie down and freeze again, conveying to me his unwavering certainty about the location of the odor. This effective communication strategy allowed me to precisely determine the odor's location.

During this particular moment, Stevie understood that wearing the harness, rather than the service dog vest, indicated that it was time to search for human remains odors. It became apparent that he led the way rather than me guiding him. Stevie would immediately prepare himself for the search when I grasped his harness, displaying an unwavering determination. It was as though nothing could deter him from his task.

As I prepared to release him to begin the search, I would utter *Busca*, which translates to "find" in Catalan, my first language. It is worth mentioning that Stevie had been trained in multiple languages. Being trilingual, I found incorporating various languages into my dog training routines enjoyable. In this case, I chose to use *Busca* because I had already used the phrase "find it" when instructing him to search for his toy. Interestingly, Stevie seemed to instinctively associate the word *busca* with the act of searching for cadavers, as wearing the harness served as the primary indication of our purpose.

Training Stevie for search and detection was a unique experience that deviated from the usual systematic approach. Instead of following the conventional method of introducing additional boxes without any odor, I had to adapt the training process with Stevie.

In Stevie's case, I would position the sample with the brick in different locations within the search area. This allowed Stevie to associate the specific odor with the task of locating it. To reinforce his understanding, I had additional bricks present that did not carry any odors, ensuring that Stevie recognized the distinction and focused solely on the target odors.

As the training progressed, I gradually introduced more challenges to make the searches increasingly demanding for Stevie. I strategically placed distractions such as dog toys, food, socks, and various objects that I believed would capture his attention. However, to my surprise, Stevie remained remarkably unfazed by the distractions. When he was on a mission to find cadaver odor, he exhibited an unwavering determination that seemed almost mechanical, reminiscent of the iconic Energizer Bunny. Stevie's focus and commitment were unparalleled; nothing could deter him from his objective. He displayed a relentless drive that kept him going and going, tirelessly searching until he successfully located the target odor.

One of the times I trained Stevie outdoors, I made a beginner mistake as a dog trainer. It was my first time working with a search-and-rescue detection dog, and I was training alone. Despite feeling a bit embarrassed, I'll share what happened.

On that day, my training plan involved having Stevie search a large open grass area first, followed by a smaller area where the odor would be hidden beneath the ground, about an inch deep. To provide a strong scent, I decided to use a rotten tooth with some tissue still attached. I placed the tooth near a group of flowers in the middle of the search area, allowing me to locate it if Stevie couldn't find it. Additionally, I walked around the search area to eliminate any trails or traces that Stevie could detect and follow to the tooth.

With preparations complete, Stevie and I followed our training routine. I released him off-leash since it was a spacious area without obstacles. I tried to stay near him but at a sufficient distance to avoid interrupting his search. When Stevie was about fifteen feet away from the source (the hidden tooth), he began displaying changes in behavior and indicators that he had detected the odor, even though he didn't know the exact location. He slowed down, nosing the ground, clearly following the scent cone.

You might be wondering, what is a scent cone? A scent cone, also known as an odor cone, refers to the dispersion pattern of odor molecules in the air emitted from the source (in this case, the tooth). When an odor is released, it spreads out in a cone shape, gradually expanding and dissipating as it moves away from the source. This creates a three-dimensional region in the air, resembling a cone, with the source located at the apex. Within the scent cone, the odor concentration is highest near the source, diminishing as the distance increases. The cone widens as it extends farther, covering a larger area with lower odor intensity. Stevie navigated this scent cone, differentiating the scent of interest within it, tracking from areas of higher concentration to lower concentration, and ultimately locating the source, which happened to be the tooth.

And then it happened! Just as Stevie found the tooth, he swallowed it! I couldn't help but voice my concern, saying, "Stevie, don't!" Unfortunately, I was unable to stop him from eating it. I could imagine how tasty the tooth must have seemed to him. It was difficult to be mad at him because he had completed his job of finding and indicating the location of the odor source. The fault was entirely mine. Experienced trainers always place odors in containers to prevent damage, contamination, or, in this case, a dog like Stevie eating it.

You may wonder how a dog can detect an odor source if it's in a container. This process is known as odor permeation, which involves the passage of odorous compounds through a material or barrier, becoming detectable on the other side. It's a fascinating aspect of scent detection.

That day, I certainly learned my lesson. I vowed never to place odor samples without a container or barrier. In roles like police dogs, the tooth could hold substantial evidence, and I would have had to monitor Stevie's feces until the tooth passed through. Luckily, that wasn't the case, and I knew Stevie wouldn't have any issues eliminating the tooth. No, I didn't search for it either. I had many other teeth to use, so losing one wasn't a big deal.

Chapter 7

Getting Ready For Certification

I felt a sense of accomplishment as Stevie, and I prepared for the human remains detection certification. We were confident in our training and abilities and ready to put our skills to the test. The certification testing was scheduled to take place in North Carolina, which required us to embark on a long drive from our home in Florida to reach our destination.

On our journey, I decided to divide the trip by staying at a hotel for one night. This plan brought back vivid memories of Stevie's very first hotel stay. At that point, Stevie was still adjusting to life as a working dog, and every new setting was a learning experience filled with its own set of challenges for both of us.

Stevie was just five months old when he first experienced an overnight stay in a hotel. During that stay, his curiosity was palpable. He busily sniffed at the air, eagerly picking up a variety of smells. The distinctive odors of cleaning agents, lingering scents from past guests, and the particular fragrance of the hotel itself all combined to create a rich sensory patchwork for Stevie to dissect and interpret. Alert to his surroundings, Stevie would also lift his head and direct his ears toward any sounds that captured his attention, showing his keen interest in the novel environment. Upon entering a hotel room for the first time, Stevie was eager to explore our hotel room. His nose twitched excitedly as a bouquet of scents hit him the tangy odor of lemon-scented cleaning spray, a hint of floral air freshener, and the mysterious, lingering essence of someone who possibly enjoyed a tuna sandwich in bed.

With a wagging tail and ears perked in curious attention, Stevie set off on his recon mission. He trotted confidently toward where his nose told him there was a sofa, but his whiskers brushed against something unexpectedly soft and fluffy. In his determination, Stevie nosed forward into what turned out to be an extremely decorative and rather large potted plant. Unfazed by the sudden rustle of leaves, he decided to conquer it by proudly lifting his leg a gesture promptly interrupted by my startled calls!

After being gently steered away from the foliage and reassured that it was not, in fact, the designated bathroom, Stevie continued. He sniffed his way to the bed, head tilted high to capture more intriguing odors. Perhaps due to his courageous foliage encounter, he mistook the height of the bed and attempted an athletic leap onto the luxurious mattress. Unfortunately, his calculations were slightly off; instead of landing gracefully on top, he managed to bump his head lightly against the side and tumble into a neat roll against it, ending up snugly between the bed and the nightstand.

I rushed over, but there was no need for concern. Stevie was lying on his back, four paws in the air, happily wagging his tail as he embraced this perfectly snug nook. In moments, familiar snores began to replace the sound of his tail thumps. Stevie had inadvertently discovered the coziness of his doggy-sized den in the fancy hotel room. His spirit undampened by this slight miscalculation, Stevie proved that joy finds a way, even if it means finding delight in a misadventure of blind exploration.

On this trip to North Carolina, Stevie was a little more than a year old. As we entered the hotel room, I used our cue word, "room," to let Stevie know that this was a different setting, a new environment for him to explore and adjust to. Despite his blindness, Stevie adapted remarkably quickly. Within minutes, he seemed right at home, scampering around the beds and furniture with youthful energy. His blindness became inconspicuous as he navigated the room effortlessly as if he had been there countless times before. Stevie would commit the space to memory, understanding the boundaries and layout, and creating a mental map that facilitates easier navigation for subsequent movements.

It was heartwarming to see Stevie embracing his surroundings and enjoying the novelty of a hotel room. Along with his playful antics, an air of confidence emanated from him, reminding me of the growth and progress we had made together on our journey as a search-and-rescue team.

The hotel stay provided crucial downtime for both of us, allowing us to recharge and mentally prepare for the upcoming certification tests. I meticulously reviewed our training notes, going over the specific scenarios we would encounter during the testing process.

As we settled down for the night, I pondered our shared journey and the bond we had formed. From the early stages of training when Stevie was a puppy, uncertain and dependent on me, to now, when he had become a confident and capable partner, our connection had deepened with every training session and successful find. I couldn't help but feel grateful for the opportunity to work with such a remarkable dog.

With the hotel room now filled with anticipation and excitement, we drifted off to sleep, eager for the challenges and triumphs that awaited us in the days ahead. The next morning, we would continue our journey, arriving in North Carolina ready to showcase the skills and dedication that had brought us this far.

To our surprise, at the certification location in North Carolina, they were performing some blind searches.

As Stevie and I joined the training sessions at the certification location, I was filled with a mix of excitement and apprehension. This was an opportunity to test our abilities in a new and unpredictable environment, something I had never experienced before. The fact that I did not know the location of the scent source made it even more challenging but also more authentic. It was as if we were going into a real-life search mission, unaware of what we would encounter.

In the past, when I trained at home alone, I would always hide the scent source myself. It was a controlled environment where I knew exactly where the odor was located. While it had been useful for training purposes, I knew deep down that it wasn't truly preparing us for the complexities of real-world situations. In the real world, I wouldn't have the luxury of knowing the exact hiding spot of a scent source. Therefore, the blind search exercises were critical for pushing our skills to the next level.

During a blind search, someone else hides the scent source. It could be tucked away in a room, hidden among various objects, or concealed in a crowded space. As the handler, I had to completely rely on Stevie's abilities without providing any cues or guidance. I couldn't use my voice, gestures, or any form of communication to direct him toward the target odor. This was a true test of his independent detection capabilities.

Blind searches allowed us to assess Stevie's scent detection proficiency and readiness for real-world tasks. It wasn't just about finding the scent source but executing the search without any prior guidance. Handlers often unknowingly influence their dogs in these scenarios, inadvertently leading them toward the target odor. But in a blind search, this was not possible. Stevie couldn't rely on my visual cues, but he could pick up on subtle signals such as changes in my breathing or energy level. These subtle cues became his lifeline, guiding him without me knowing I was doing it.

The significance of blind searches couldn't be overstated. They provided invaluable insights into Stevie's reliability, accuracy, and independence as a working dog. The results of these exercises would determine whether he was truly prepared for operational deployment. This was our chance to prove that Stevie was not just a well-trained dog but a proficient and highly capable asset in the world of scent detection.

As I prepared myself for the blind search exercises, I couldn't help but feel a surge of pride and anticipation. This was a pivotal moment in our journey together, and I was eager to witness Stevie's abilities shining in this challenging and uncharted territory.

We embarked on our blind search journey, exploring various environments ranging from expansive parking lots to dense forests and towering warehouses. Each new session presented its unique challenges, but one particular search remains etched in my memory to this day. It took place in a massive conference room, and what unfolded during that session continues to astound me.

Stevie and I were tasked with searching two separate conference rooms, each potentially containing a hidden odor or perhaps none at all. The first room resembled a presentation hall, with rows of chairs stretching across ten rows. The final part of the room featured a captivating scenario, with small rugs scattered beneath armchairs. Similar rugs were placed strategically throughout the room. The second room, on the other hand, had a more formal setup, boasting a grand table surrounded by chairs.

Armed with the knowledge of our mission and a strategy in mind, I headed to the car to retrieve my trusty companion. Once Stevie was secured in his harness, we confidently entered the first search area the room with the chairs and scenario. Considering the potential obstacles, I chose to keep Stevie on a leash for this search. It was clear that this exercise would require my guidance to navigate the chairs effectively.

We began our search at the farthest end of the room, away from the scenario. Slowly, we walked around the entire space, leaving an intriguing scene for later investigation. After completing a thorough walkthrough, we systematically managed the rows of chairs. I walked backward, leading the way as Stevie followed the sound of my footsteps while diligently examining the areas we passed. As we progressed beyond the third row, we picked up the pace, and Stevie quickly grasped the pattern of the search. His behavior remained consistent, indicating that there was no hidden odor in the rows of chairs we had searched. It was now time to turn our attention to the scenario.

Guiding Stevie to the stairs, I observed a noticeable change in his demeanor. He began pulling me forward with increasing excitement as we reached the scenario. I maintained a firm grip on the leash, aware that this area contained fewer obstacles he could detect before colliding with them. Stevie proceeded with deliberate steps, his nose almost glued to the ground. Intense sniffing sounds filled the air as he dedicatedly investigated every nook and cranny. It was an awe-inspiring sight to witness his dedication and focus.

At the second armchair within the scenario, Stevie abruptly stopped, fixating on the rug beneath it. His tail wagged with enthusiasm, revealing his excitement. Without hesitation, he lay down, indicating that he had successfully detected the location of the odor's source. At that moment, despite not seeing anything on the rug, I had complete faith in Stevie's abilities. After all, he possessed an extraordinary sense of smell, far more powerful than my own. Confirming our suspicions, the trainer who had hidden the odor validated Stevie's findings there was indeed a trace of human remains on that rug. I rewarded Stevie with a delectable steak, showering him with praise for his exceptional performance. "Great job, my sweet boy. You are truly an amazing dog. Let's approach our second search with the same confidence, knowing that we are in control."

Moving on to the second room, Stevie confidently told me no cadaver odors were present. Once again, his instincts were correct, reaffirming his incredible competence as a scent-detection dog.

As the training sessions concluded, during the debrief, the trainer complimented Stevie's prowess, hailing him as extraordinary among a group of twenty dogs. Only Stevie and one other canine companion had successfully identified the rug with the hidden odor. The startling fact that the carpet had been cleaned three years prior to being stained with human blood further highlighted Stevie's remarkable abilities. This training session left me in awe of the incredible power of a dog's nose and marked yet another milestone in our journey.

"Stevie, after this training session, I have full confidence that we are ready for the certification testing," I exclaimed, affectionately rubbing his belly. Each milestone we achieved together showcased Stevie's incredible talents, paving the way for the final stages of preparation and the exhilarating days ahead leading up to our ultimate goal certification.

Chapter 8

Certification

Stevie and I had been preparing for our Human Remains Detection K9 Certification test for about six months, and the two-day test was filled with challenging search scenarios that truly put Stevie's abilities to the test. The intensity of the experience was a mix of nerve-wracking anticipation and exhilaration as we showcased the skills and dedication we had honed over time.

Our impending certification session was scheduled at a highly reputable canine training center in North Carolina, known for its comprehensive programs and proficient staff. Given my familiarity with this facility's highly skilled instructors and trainers, I seized the opportunity to bring Aki, my expertly trained German shepherd, known for his proficient skills in patrol duties.

The facility's robust training environment and resources presented a valuable chance for me to further Aki's expertise. With access to knowledgeable trainers at the facility, I planned to engage Aki in advanced narcotic detection exercises, allowing him to refine his ability to locate and signal the presence of illicit substances. Additionally, we would participate in man-tracking training. This would hone Aki's skills in following human scent trails, an essential capability for various law enforcement and search-and-rescue scenarios.

The combination of our certification endeavors and the additional training for Aki at this esteemed K9 training center represented a strategic approach to maximizing our visit and taking full advantage of the expertise available at this North Carolina facility.

Cadaver detection K9 teams, like ours, are valuable for search-and-rescue efforts and police work. During our certification, we faced a variety of scenarios that simulated the different situations where our skills would be required. This included searching areas where human remains were suspected to be located. For example, in the case of disaster response, such as natural disasters or mass casualty incidents, we were trained to search large areas to locate victims or deceased individuals quickly. Our role was vital in helping search-and-rescue teams prioritize their efforts and provide closure to grieving families.

One significant event that comes to mind is the Oso landslide in Washington State in 2014, where forty-three people lost their lives. The cadaver detection K9 teams were deployed to find the missing individuals who were suspected to be deceased. As part of a search-and-rescue organization in the area, Stevie and I could have been deployed. Still, the Federal Emergency Management Agency (FEMA) took charge of the situation, and they did not want volunteer search-and-rescue organizations, including ours, to have their dogs deployed. Due to specific, critical advantages, FEMA prioritizes using its certified K9 teams in disaster areas over local alternatives. These FEMA-certified teams have completed extensive training programs establishing uniformity in skills and abilities essential for effective and well-coordinated search-and-rescue efforts. In contrast, local teams often exhibit a broad range of training and experience, potentially causing inconsistency in response effectiveness. By deploying its certified teams, FEMA retains direct control and oversight, thus ensuring search-and-rescue operations proceed seamlessly and resources are used wisely and effectively.

In addition to disaster response, cadaver detection dogs also play a crucial role in crime scene investigation. Law enforcement agencies utilize these teams to assist in locating human remains and other substantial evidence at crime scenes. The K9 teams can alert their handlers to the presence of human remains, facilitating the discovery of concealed or buried body parts, clandestine graves, or remains hidden within structures. They serve as invaluable resources in forensic investigations, providing crucial assistance to law enforcement agencies and helping to solve crimes.

Furthermore, cadaver detection dogs can trail the scent of decomposing human remains over long distances. This particular application becomes relevant in cases where a missing person is believed to have died, and their body may have been moved or concealed. By following the scent trails, the K9 teams can lead investigators to the location where the body was initially present or subsequent locations where related evidence may exist. Their ability to track odors allows for more efficient searches and enhances the chances of recovering necessary evidence, providing critical assistance in resolving cases.

During our certification, Stevie and I were tested in various environments and search areas, including a vehicle, building, scattered bones, exposed find, and a primarily buried find with distractions. Now, let's explore each search area and our experiences in detail.

Before initiating any search during the certification process, the master trainer responsible for conducting the test provides a briefing about a hypothetical case. This step is taken to make the certification as realistic as possible, allowing the team to demonstrate their preparedness for real-life situations. By simulating scenarios closely resembling actual scenarios, the certification assesses the team's ability to handle various challenges and situations they may encounter effectively.

The initial search area presented a breathtaking view, resembling a picturesque painting. A sprawling meadow merged seamlessly with a dense forest, combining elements of natural beauty. However, the tranquility of the setting was in stark contrast to the grim objective of our mission: to uncover evidence hidden by a hypothetical murderer.

We were tasked with investigating a single potential location where the victim's body might have been concealed. Stevie's excitement grew evident as we stepped into the first search area, a field illuminated by the gentle morning sun. His tail wagged vigorously, reflecting his eagerness to commence our search. The warmth of the sunlight intensified our anticipation, casting a golden glow over the surroundings.

Operating within a strict thirty-minute time frame, we wasted no time initiating our exploration. Stevie unleashed and empowered by his training and expertise, assumed the lead with unwavering determination. In Stevie's meticulous fashion, he traversed the meadow and ventured deep into the encompassing forest. With his nose hovering close to the ground, he meticulously sniffed for any discernible trace, any scent that could potentially lead us to the victim.

Fifteen minutes had elapsed, yet Stevie had not indicated the presence of any significant odor. Despite his unwavering efforts, the lack of any clear olfactory signals left us confident in our assessment. We decided to declare the area clean, signifying the absence of the specific odor Stevie had been trained to detect an absence that would suggest the lack of human remains.

Informing Kylie, the master trainer overseeing our search, I relayed our findings, stating, "I must report that the area we just searched does not exhibit any odor within Stevie's detection capabilities."

Kylie, emphasizing the importance of a thorough investigation, asked if I wanted Stevie to continue exploring the surrounding area, reminding me that we still had fifteen minutes remaining. However, based on our initial findings and Stevie's exhaustive search, I remained resolute in my assessment.

"No, I declare this area is clean," I responded, my voice firm and unwavering, reflecting my confidence in our findings.

Appreciating the gravity of our statement, Kylie sought further confirmation regarding the absence of any indicators related to human remains understanding the need for absolute certainty in such investigations.

"Are you sure about its cleanliness, meaning that there is unequivocally nothing connected to human remains?" she inquired, seeking reassurance of our conclusion.

"Yes," I replied with conviction, reiterating our findings and standing by our declaration.

Recognizing our unyielding confidence and the accuracy of our search, Kylie adorned a friendly smile, confirming our assessment.

"Well done, both you and Stevie. Your thorough search has conclusively determined that this area is indeed devoid of any evidence about the hypothetical crime," she commended, conveying a blend of admiration and encouragement through her words.

After a brief break, our search certification shifted to a nearby parking lot filled with stationary cars and trailers. The master trainer informed me that this time, there were suspicions about one of the vehicles potentially being used to transport human remains. She pointed me toward the specific section of the parking lot where I was to search with the assistance of my trained companion, Stevie. I kept Stevie on a short leash as we entered the area to ensure better control and guidance.

With his remarkable skills, Stevie began meticulously inspecting the vehicles, skillfully utilizing his long, floppy ears to explore the edges of each car and his keen nose to pick up any subtle scents. As we proceeded through the lot, one car caught our attention the sixth one in line. During our investigation of this vehicle, Stevie displayed a noticeable behavior change. He abruptly halted his search and pulled me in a different direction, indicating that he had picked up something significant.

Intrigued by Stevie's sudden change in demeanor, I followed his lead. He exhibited a fascinated interest in a specific spot on the ground, clearly indicating that he had detected a trail of odor. While Stevie was eager to go underneath the cars to get closer to the source, I prioritized his safety and restrained him. At the same time, I noticed a gentle breeze blowing from the nearby trailers. Stevie's behavior shifted toward the trailers, suggesting he had detected something interesting. His actions were filled with excitement and determination. Trusting Stevie's instincts, I guided him further toward the trailers. Stevie's determination intensified as we approached, and his tail wagged faster, clearly signaling a significant discovery.

Positioning Stevie in front of the trailers, I allowed him to sniff the air and trace the scent. Stevie immediately homed in on an old, large trailer, giving his full attention to it. It seemed as though he wanted to go under the trailer, but I steered him to the other side instead. Undeterred, Stevie continued his vigorous sniffing, his tail wagging intensely yet again, indicating a significant find. He then froze in a lying-down position and started licking his lips, which served as the confirmation I sought. I knew that Stevie had identified an odor.

Before rewarding Stevie for his exceptional work, I sought confirmation from the examiner. To my satisfaction, it was confirmed that Stevie's instincts had once again proved to be accurate. Inside the trailer, we discovered an old cloth seemingly used to wrap an injured person. The fabric was now stained with human blood. Stevie's remarkable detection skills uncovered crucial evidence for our hypothetical case, further emphasizing the value of well-trained search dogs like Stevie in forensic investigations.

Due to the rising temperature, we moved the search certification indoors. Seeking relief from the scorching heat outside, we entered a warehouse for the third test scenario. The new story involved a possible murderer who had concealed a trophy from the victim among the stored furniture in the warehouse. Stevie and I prepared ourselves for the search, knowing that the temperature inside would be more tolerable.

As we entered the warehouse, a musty smell of aged furniture permeated the air. The vast expanse of rows filled with various items necessitated a slower pace for the search. To maintain control and efficiency, I again had Stevie on a six-foot leash, with me taking the lead in directing his search pattern. Walking backward in front of him, I used my fingernails to tap on specific items, indicating to Stevie which areas to investigate and ensuring his focus on the most promising areas.

We combed the entire search area, meticulously inspecting every piece of furniture. However, I started to doubt our search approach when I noticed some bones Stevie had overlooked entirely. I reminded myself that as the handler, I needed to trust Stevie's expertise in detecting cadaver odor. Sometimes, humans mistakenly believe we know better or more than our canines.

After regaining my confidence, I couldn't shake the feeling that we hadn't given enough attention to the initial section of the warehouse. Trusting my instincts, I decided to backtrack and provide Stevie another opportunity to sniff around that area thoroughly.

Returning to the starting point, Stevie's nose led him straight to a corner where a sofa with stacked boxes caught his interest. He sniffed intently around the furniture piece, clearly wanting to climb the sofa and investigate further. Understanding his eagerness, I helped him onto the sofa to observe him closely and determine how best to assist him. With his front paws on the sofa's back, Stevie directed his attention toward a nearby clothing cabinet just behind it. His sniffing became intense, focusing on the openings of the cabinet's drawers. However, the proximity of the chest to the back of the sofa hindered his ability to explore the bottom drawers fully.

As Stevie attempted to jump off the back of the sofa to get closer to the cabinet drawers, I quickly intervened, calling out to him to stop and prevent any potential injuries from the unsafe landing. Assessing the situation, I searched for the best approach to guide him toward the cabinet and allow for further investigation. Before proceeding, I sought permission from Kylie and informed her of my confidence in an odor source being present in the drawer.

Kylie granted permission, stating, "Yes, you can move the furniture if you believe it will assist your dog in concluding the investigation of that area." Another handler undergoing certification was in the warehouse, and I requested his assistance holding Stevie while I moved the furniture. Stevie could sense that I was not holding the leash as I began pushing the pieces, causing him to pull hard in my direction. I used a soothing voice to calm him down, reassuring him, saying, "It's okay, my sweet boy. You are okay."

With the furniture rearranged, Stevie could now thoroughly investigate the cabinet from top to bottom. Retaking hold of Stevie's leash, I guided him to the cabinet, and within seconds, he began sniffing the drawers, starting from the bottom and following the scent trail to the third one. He engaged in an intense sniffing session with his front paws on the cabinet, and Stevie froze in that position. Because he was licking his lips, I instructed him to "show me," using his nose, he pointed to the opening of the third drawer before freezing again.

At that moment, I couldn't help but think, *Wow, my boy is exceptional!* Kylie confirmed that a bone had been hidden at the bottom of the third drawer. While debriefing about the search, Kylie informed me that in a real case, Stevie's behavioral change near the sofa by the cabinet would have been enough evidence for the police to search inside the cabinet without Stevie's final indication of the find. She also mentioned that these certification searches are often utilized for training purposes, and completing them as we did was a commendable achievement.

As the sun began to set on the first day of testing, a sense of accomplishment and pride washed over us. I knew that Stevie's talent and training had carried us through successfully. With each challenge we faced together, our bond was growing stronger.

After all the hard work, it was time for Stevie to rest. We returned to the hotel, where I treated him to a nourishing dinner. As a reward for his exceptional performance, I let him indulge in his favorite chew bone, which he enthusiastically enjoyed. Stevie slept soundly, utterly unaware of the nerves that consumed me as I anticipated our final day of testing. Despite my anxiety, I could not deny that Stevie had excelled so far, and I was determined not to let any distractions hinder our success.

On the second day, we approached the certification test with renewed determination. The morning air was cool, but we expected it to heat up as the day went on, presenting additional challenges.

The first search area was a large field and forest divided by an elementary school. The scenario involved a hypothetical murderer moving a body for burial. Stevie and I positioned ourselves at the starting point, ready to begin the search. The wind worked in our favor, helping Stevie detect odors more effectively.

With a thirty-minute timer ticking, we started the search. Stevie led the way on a long line while I followed, guiding me within the search area. Our firm bond and understanding of each other's cues proved invaluable in maximizing our efficiency.

Throughout the search, Stevie diligently explored the area, using his nose to sniff out any hidden odor. The heat started to affect Stevie's stamina as the temperature rose with the sun. I made sure he stayed hydrated and gave him short breaks to keep him comfortable.

Toward the end of the search, Stevie's behavior suddenly changed as he investigated an area near a line of dense trees. His heightened interest was evident, and he crawled toward the bushes, sniffing intensely at the ground. It was clear that he had picked up on something important.

He quickly moved to a specific tree, sniffing deeply into the trunk. He stopped sniffing and froze with his front paws on the trunk. At that moment, I realized Stevie had detected an odor on the tree. Despite not lying down as usual to indicate a find, Stevie's position made it clear that there was an odor source on the tree. Wanting further confirmation, I asked Stevie to show it to me. He moved away, got down on the ground again, and then sniffed the air while standing on his back legs under the tree's branches. He repeated this a few times before returning to the trunk, placing his front paws on it, and freezing in position. I trusted Stevie's instincts and believed in his detection skills.

I informed Kylie, "There is an odor around or in the tree. I can't pinpoint the exact location, but I know it's nearby."

Kylie was impressed and confirmed, "You have an impressive dog. There is indeed something on the tree."

When the examiner asked about the search, I explained my confidence in Stevie's behavior. Even though I couldn't see anything, I knew that an odor he had been trained to detect was present or nearby. The examiner smiled and pointed to the lower branches of the tree. "Look up; you'll see a few strands of brown hair entangled in the leaves, cleverly hiding in plain sight."

"As I always say, a good handler must trust their dog and not assume they know better just because they're human. After all, the dog has a nose!"

After the successful search, we rested and allowed Stevie some well-deserved relaxation in his comfortable crate. I ensured he had access to plenty of water.

The second search occurred in an area filled with short bushes, making it denser and more challenging for us. The scenario involved a woman who had been missing for approximately ten days, with suspicions that she may have passed away during that time.

As always, Stevie was eager and enthusiastic to get to work. We began the search with the wind blowing toward us, giving Stevie the advantage of scent direction. His innate hunting instincts took over as he diligently scoured the area.

Suddenly, Stevie pulled me toward a dense, shrubby area with determination. I followed his lead as he crawled through the bushes, sniffing the ground with heightened intensity and excitement. Since it was a safe environment for him to be off-leash, I allowed him to conduct a free search. Stevie thoroughly investigated the bushes, circling them multiple times in excitement. It was clear that he had found something, and I knew he was close. After a few moments, Stevie indicated the presence of an odor. When I asked him to show me, he put his nose to the ground and froze in that position.

Seeking confirmation, I turned to Kylie before rewarding Stevie. I informed her, "There is something beneath the dirt."

Kylie responded, "Marina, you are correct. Stevie has found the source. He discovered a hidden treasure buried under the bushes. Well done!" Kylie went on to explain, "Stevie located an amputated foot buried approximately eight inches deep. The foot was donated by a friend who had diabetes and had lost his foot due to the disease. It was used as training material for search-and-rescue organizations to train their cadaver dogs."

We were nearing the end of our certification searches, with just one remaining. This final search took place in two apartments, specifically small studio-style units. Our objective was to locate a murder weapon a knife.

In both cases, I initially walked Stevie around the apartments on a leash, and then I allowed him to conduct a free search independently. Like our experiences in hotel rooms, Stevie quickly grasped the layout of each studio and conducted a thorough search independently.

After completing the search in the first studio, Stevie approached me at the front door, indicating that he had finished searching. The studio was clear of any cadaver odors.

In the second studio, we followed the same search procedure as before. However, this time, there were distractions, such as food and animal blood on the carpet, intended to divert the dog's attention. Stevie remained focused and ignored these distractions. He showed particular interest in the bed, sniffing intensely beneath the mattress and attempting to reach under it. Eventually, Stevie indicated that an odor source was beneath the mattress by lying down and positioning his nose under it.

Glancing at Kylie, I noticed her trying to hold back a laugh at Stevie's amusing behavior. Her smile confirmed that Stevie had once again proven correct. After rewarding Stevie for his excellent work, Kylie retrieved a knife from under the bed with traces of blood on it.

As the certification ended, the master trainer recognized Stevie, the blind dog, as one of the top performers in the search.

During the assessment, Kylie, the master trainer, observed Stevie with keen attention and recognized several noteworthy capabilities that Stevie exhibited. First and foremost, Stevie's ability to pinpoint and signal the presence of target scents was remarkably accurate. His exceptional olfactory acuity more than compensated for his lack of sight, allowing him to detect scents with impressive precision. Upon locating the intended odor, Stevie consistently communicated this discovery to me, the handler, through a specifically trained behavior lying down to indicate that he had found the scent.

Kylie took note of Stevie's responsiveness to my vocal instructions and hand signals. Despite his blindness, he could follow my commands with precision, demonstrating that he could stay focused on the tasks and work productively without visual cues. This responsiveness showed Stevie could operate effectively in a working environment, even without sight.

Moreover, Kylie observed that as Stevie moved through various settings and over different surfaces, he didn't just rely on his heightened sense of smell. He also used his sense of touch and acute hearing to understand and adapt to new environments, all while concentrating on detecting scents.

Notably, despite the challenge his blindness could have presented, Stevie employed a search technique that was both deliberate and systematic. This reflected the depth of his training, where he had learned to methodically cover areas in search of scents. Kylie could see that

Stevie's search patterns were guided by a strong learning and practice foundation, allowing him to work as efficiently as his sighted counterparts.

Kylie summarized her observations by noting that Stevie's training had been comprehensive and effective. Stevie's proficiency, systematic approach, and the strong working bond between him and me demonstrated that he was qualified and could excel as a scent detection dog, even without the benefit of vision.

Stevie and two other dogs were the only ones to achieve a perfect 100 percent success rate; three others passed, and one did not pass.

Stevie's extraordinary sense of smell had once again showcased his immense value in search and rescue. As we looked ahead to future adventures, I couldn't help but revel in the knowledge that, with Stevie by my side, there were no limits to what we could accomplish.

Returning home, we were greeted warmly by our loving family and friends. Stevie had charmed everyone he met and seamlessly transitioned into his roles as a cherished family companion, service dog, and dedicated search-and-rescue partner.

Several days following our return to Florida, I was pleasantly greeted by an official piece of mail a certificate of achievement from the National Tactical Police Dog Association (NTPDA). This document confirmed that Stevie and I had triumphantly met the rigorous certification standards set by the NTPDA in the specialized field of human remains detection. It was a tangible testament to the hard work, dedication, and synergy between Stevie and myself throughout our training.

In a gesture of pride and reverence for the accomplishment, I procured a frame for the prestigious certificate. Once framed, I carefully placed it on display in our living room, ensuring it held a prominent position. I wanted this token of recognition to be one of the first things someone noticed upon entering our home. The certificate, now displayed for all to see, served as a silent yet powerful testament to Stevie's exceptional abilities and our collective achievement. It was important to me that friends, family, and visitors alike could witness the documented success of Stevie, a remarkable dog who had overcome his visual limitations to excel in a demanding field. Each glance at the framed certificate reminded us of our bond and the milestones we had reached together as an unbeatable team.

By completing the Human Remains Detection (HRD) certification tests with Stevie, I've gained official recognition of our joint capabilities in this intricate domain. This achievement has unlocked various opportunities and responsibilities.

One significant avenue now accessible to us is contributing to criminal investigations. With certification, we are qualified to assist law enforcement in locating human remains, a service that can be instrumental in case resolution and providing much-needed closure to the families of missing individuals.

Additionally, our certification qualifies us to participate actively in search-and-rescue missions. In the aftermath of disasters such as earthquakes, tsunamis, floods, or other catastrophic events, HRD dogs are an essential asset. Our role can be pivotal in finding individuals affected by such tragic circumstances, aiding in the relief and recovery.

Beyond fieldwork, our expertise and proven proficiency allow us to engage in educational initiatives. This could involve delivering informative presentations and dynamic demonstrations at educational institutions, community gatherings, or specialized training seminars. These engagements are crucial for sharing knowledge about the significant contributions of HRD dogs within law enforcement circles and search-and-rescue operations, heightening public understanding and appreciation of this field.

However, with the accolade of professional recognition comes the duty to uphold and exceed the established performance and professional ethics standards. Engaging in ongoing training and regular re-certification is imperative to ensure our skills remain sharp and up to date. Keeping informed about emerging techniques and the evolving body of knowledge in HRD work is also essential to ensure we can continue offering superior services in human remains detection and maintain our standing as certified practitioners.

Chapter 9

Work Well Done

Freshly certified as a human remains detection K9 team, Stevie and I were excited and excited. We had completed our training and were officially ready to use our skills to assist the community. Little did we know that our first assignment would become a testament to Stevie's remarkable abilities and unwavering determination.

Shortly after our certification, we started our drive back to Florida. Exhausted from the intense week of training, the road stretched out before us, offering a much-needed respite. It was a peaceful journey until my phone rang, interrupting the tranquility of the drive. It was an urgent call from Janet.

"Marina, where are you?" Janet's voice crackled with urgency. "I hope you're not too far down your drive. There's a local police department in North Carolina that is in desperate need of Human Remain Detection K9 teams. They require immediate assistance."

My heart raced as I listened to Janet's words. This was an unexpected turn of events. We had only just become certified, and now there was a real-life situation calling for our specialized skills. Without hesitation, I assured her, "Of course, I would love to help, and I'm not far. I've been driving for a little over an hour. Let me turn around, and I should be there soon."

The adrenaline coursed through my veins as I navigated the car with precision, swiftly making my way back to the training facility. I couldn't shake off the excitement of being called into action so soon after our certification. Deep down, I knew we were ready for this challenge.

Turning to my faithful canine companions, Stevie and Aki, who were comfortably nestled in the back seat, I shared the news. "Stevie, Aki, a police department is requesting our help! Let's show them just how good we are." The dogs perked up, their ears and wagging tails expressing their understanding and shared enthusiasm.

Arriving at the training facility, I joined Janet, who had managed to gather a total of four teams, including herself, to assist in the search. The other K9 team consisted of German shepherds, making Stevie the only medium-sized dog among them. However, I had unwavering confidence in Stevie's abilities and knew that size wouldn't hinder our success. We were all skilled and determined to make a difference.

Before departing for the scene, Janet gathered all the handlers, assigning each team a helper. During searches, it's essential to have someone accompanying the K9 team, easing the burden on the handler and allowing them to focus entirely on the search. Janet introduced me to Amanda, one of the dog trainer interns, who would be my trusted shadow throughout this operation.

The anticipation and excitement grew as Amanda and I assembled the necessary equipment. We joined the other teams and embarked on our mission together, heading toward the location where the police awaited our arrival. The gravity of the situation held us in its grip, and the sense of purpose that propelled us forward was palpable.

The drive to the scene was filled with a mix of emotions. We were anxious to assist in a matter of utmost importance, yet there was also a sense of trepidation about what lay ahead. The details of the situation were still unknown to us, leaving room for uncertainty. But as we neared our destination, those concerns were eclipsed by an unwavering determination to bring closure to those in need.

As we arrived at the scene, the flashing lights of the police cars created an atmosphere of urgency. The air was tense as we parked our vehicles according to the officers' instructions. The location we were about to search bordered a bustling road, its constant traffic serving as a backdrop to the unfolding drama. Stepping out of our cars, we left our furry partners behind, their presence palpable even in their absence.

We gathered around the sergeant and other officers, awaiting the briefing that would give us a clearer understanding of the situation. The weight of responsibility settled upon us as the sergeant relayed the harrowing details of a fatal car accident that had occurred the previous night. Three lives had been tragically lost, leaving only the driver, their fate unknown. Desperate to locate the missing driver, the police had contacted us, hoping that our unique expertise and specially trained dogs could shed light on his whereabouts.

Family and relatives had been contacted, but no one had seen or heard from the driver since the accident; the hours ticked by relentlessly, surpassing the twenty-hour mark since the crash. The police considered the possibility that the disoriented and maybe injured driver may have stumbled into the nearby woods. He could be lost and unable to move, or worse, his life extinguished. The need for cadaver dogs became increasingly imperative.

Janet, our seasoned leader, conversed with the sergeant, discussing our available teams and explaining that we already had established partnerships. However, radios were requested to facilitate seamless coordination and ensure effective communication among all search parties. After a brief exchange, Janet was informed that four distinct areas within the forested region required our meticulous search efforts. These areas posed similar challenges, with dense vegetation and uneven terrain hindering our progress.

Assigning each team to a designated area, Janet handed out the radios and gave us essential instructions before sending us off. The gravity of the situation weighed heavily on our minds as we prepared to venture into the unknown, driven by a relentless determination to uncover the truth and bring closure to grieving loved ones.

Returning to my vehicle, I could sense Stevie's and Aki's anticipation and eagerness. They were aware that something significant was unfolding. Beyond the visual spectacle of numerous police cars, the dogs could discern the heightened energy and buzz surrounding us. In their respective crates in the back of my SUV, Stevie awaited his moment to shine, unaware of the emotional weight his delicate nose would carry as he embarked on his first official mission as certified human remains detection K9.

Ensuring we had all our necessary equipment, I took a moment to collect my thoughts, steeling myself for the challenges that lay ahead. With a deep breath, I released my loyal and eager partner, Stevie, from his crate, his tail wagging with uncontainable excitement. As I fastened his harness and secured his working gear, I offered him words of encouragement, grateful for our unwavering bond.

As I busily prepared Stevie, I was unaware of the sergeant's presence until he unexpectedly appeared at my side. His distressed expression and the anguish in his voice instantly caught my attention. In a tone of disbelief, he questioned Stevie's suitability for the task at hand and expressed doubt that a small brown dog could fulfill the role of a working dog, unlike the other dog in the car. Before I could comprehend what had just transpired, the sergeant continued, emphasizing the gravity of the situation and urging me to recognize its importance.

A whirlwind of thoughts swirled in my mind. Was the sergeant's comment influenced by my gender or ethnicity? Or was it simply a result of his ignorance that different breeds can excel as search-and-rescue dogs? These questions raced through my head as I prepared to respond. However, I knew that maintaining composure was crucial. Taking a deep breath, I mustered my thoughts and chose my words carefully before replying.

"Sir, I assure you that I am treating this situation with utmost seriousness, just like everyone else involved. Stevie, here is my certified K9 partner, fully capable of performing the necessary tasks," I calmly replied, attempting to address any misconceptions. Wanting to challenge the sergeant's biased assumptions, I added, "Sir, it's important to remember that one should never judge a book by its cover."

Still brimming with confidence in Stevie's training and instincts, we headed into the forest together. The terrain posed significant challenges, with dense shrubs and obstructing trees impeding our progress. Undeterred, Stevie eagerly launched into the search, demonstrating unwavering determination. His acute sense of smell diligently dissected the environment as he tirelessly scoured the area, seeking any trace of the scent of human remains.

Despite the sergeant's initial skepticism based on Stevie's appearance, I remained resolute in my faith in his abilities. Together, we ventured further, navigating the demanding landscape with unwavering resolve. Stevie's commitment to the search grew stronger with each step, evidence of his impeccable training and unwavering focus. His diligent nose tirelessly detected even the faintest scent, driving us forward in our mission to locate any possible traces of human presence.

Before embarking on our search, Amanda and I carefully examined the map of the expansive area we were tasked with covering. Most of the area was densely covered in forest, with several creeks running through it. The vegetation was thick, and there were no clear paths to follow. Unfortunately, there was no wind that day, which could have aided Stevie in detecting and tracking any potential scent of a cadaver.

After considering our options, we decided that employing a grid pattern would be the most effective method for searching the area. The grid pattern is a widely used technique for systematically covering large areas, minimizing the chances of overlooking any possible scents. Amanda held the map and guided Stevie and I advanced slowly through the front, impeded by the dense vegetation.

To navigate through the thick areas, I led Stevie, ensuring that he avoided the most impassable sections. In instances of particularly dense vegetation, I would position myself in front of him while he closely followed behind, attuned to the movement of my feet. During these moments, I walked slowly, allowing Stevie to overcome any small obstacles on the ground. If we encountered larger obstacles like fallen trees, I would tell Stevie, "Big jump," prompting him to touch the trunk with his nose, raise his front legs, and leap over it.

Although it may appear that Stevie was not actively searching for the odor during these instances, he was indeed on high alert.

While maneuvering through a cluster of bushes, Stevie abruptly stopped following my lead and attempted to veer in a different direction.

However, the path he sought was nearly impossible due to the dense and unyielding vegetation. Worried about his safety, I held him closer and turned to Amanda for assistance.

"Amanda, I need your help determining the best way for us to proceed in the direction Stevie wants to go. His behavior change suggests he has detected an odor," I urgently said.

Amanda surveyed our surroundings and consulted the map before signaling that if we retraced our steps a few feet, there was a small opening that we could pass through. And so, we reversed our course, with me soothing Stevie as he persistently yearned to explore the impossible terrain we had just left behind. He couldn't comprehend why I was redirecting him away from his desired direction.

Upon reaching the small opening Amanda had discovered, I allowed Stevie to take the lead again. Without hesitation, his nose began alternating between the ground and the air. He guided us toward a nearby creek, where he intently sniffed the damp sand and mud. Following the edge of the creek, which had less vegetation, Stevie became even more determined. Amanda and I joined him in closely inspecting the ground, hoping to uncover something significant. Then, we noticed what appeared to be dots, possibly indicating the presence of blood, in an area covered in leaves.

Instantly, Stevie pulled me forcefully toward the spot where we believed we had found blood. Thus, fueled by his excitement and unwavering resolve, we followed his lead. Stevie was on the trail of the scent; he had indeed detected it. The shared realization among the three of us filled us with incredible enthusiasm.

"Wow, look at him go! It's truly amazing to witness Stevie pick up the scent of the blood and track it," exclaimed Amanda, observing Stevie's remarkable skills in action for the first time. While she knew he was talented at detecting, seeing him in action was awe-inspiring.

Amid the difficult vegetation and numerous obstacles, it became evident that Stevie was successfully trailing a scent. I remained closely behind him, assisting him in maneuvering through tight spots. We sometimes even had to crawl under bushes when there were no other viable paths to maintain Stevie's scent trail. Despite the challenges, we were fully committed to helping Stevie locate the missing individual. Together, we navigated obstacles and treacherous terrain. Stevie led us through overgrown bushes, under fallen trees, and across creeks for over an hour, showing no signs of fatigue. His unwavering determination and focus propelled us forward as we relentlessly pursued the source of the scent, never wavering in our efforts.

"Marina, we are approaching a busy road; I will let you know if Stevie keeps going that way," Amanda instructed me as we neared the sound of approaching cars. Despite the noise, we continued to follow Stevie. After pushing through some dense undergrowth, we reached the road. Stevie showed a strong desire to continue, as if he wanted to cross the busy street. Amanda and I assessed the situation and quickly realized it was unsafe to venture onto the road without assistance from the police. We decided to contact the sergeant using our radios.

"This is Marina, one of the handlers. My dog has been following a potential trail of blood. We are currently near a busy road, and Stevie seems determined to cross it. Based on his excitement and pulling behavior, it is clear that he is still tracking the scent. We need guidance on what to do next," I relayed over the radio.

"This is the sergeant. Could you repeat your message? I couldn't understand what you said," came the response. Perplexed by the poor reception, I repeated my message, hoping for a better connection this time. However, the sergeant still struggled to comprehend my words and requested another repetition.

As I looked at Amanda, my frustration was evident. "I know I get nervous when speaking on the radio, but I believe my message was clear. Let's chalk it up to a bad signal, and perhaps he can't hear me well through his radio." I expressed my frustration.

Amanda kindly offered to speak to the sergeant on the radio, and I agreed, not wanting to compound my frustration. As expected, when Amanda relayed the same message, the sergeant understood it on the first attempt. "I heard you loud and clear now," he confirmed.

I won't elaborate on my thoughts about the sergeant then, as they were not particularly pleasant. Let's say I chose to keep those sentiments to myself.

The sergeant inquired if we could see what was on the other side of the road. Amanda informed him that, according to the map and our observations, there were buildings that appeared to be stores or restaurants. She provided him with the exact locations where we were stationed. The sergeant advised us to wait at our current position and refrain from crossing the road. He was going to investigate the buildings across from us.

While awaiting further instructions from the sergeant, I decided to remove Stevie's harness in hopes that he would no longer be fixated on crossing the road and instead focus on following the scent trail. Anticipating his confusion, I also rewarded him, acknowledging his excellent work. Although we had no validation from the police or anyone else that Stevie's trail was indeed connected to the blood trail from the car accident, I trusted Stevie. I believed in his abilities, and deep down, I knew he was on the right track. That's why I rewarded him with a few pieces of steak. Stevie eagerly received the reward, and his pulling toward the road ceased.

As I praised Stevie, the police informed us that a patrol car would pick us up while other officers investigated the nearby restaurants. Once inside the patrol car, the officer revealed that one of the restaurants had had a visitor the previous day a disheveled man covered in blood who had approached them seeking a phone. The officer promised to gather more information and update us accordingly.

Amanda and I exchanged joyful smiles. "Stevie did it," Amanda exclaimed with delight, reflecting our shared happiness and pride in Stevie's accomplishments.

We regrouped with the other K9 teams, where Janet provided us with an update regarding the driver. The police had learned that the driver had taken a similar path through the woods as we did, eventually making their way to a restaurant where they sought to use a phone. It was later discovered that the driver was actually evading the police. At the restaurant, another person arrived and picked up the driver. Thankfully, the restaurant's outdoor cameras captured this interaction, providing valuable information for the police's investigation. With this newfound evidence, the police possessed leads for further investigation and apprehending the driver. Our role in the situation was now complete.

After returning to the car and removing Stevie's harness, we were approached by the sergeant once again, but this time, his expression was filled with regret. He hesitantly began, "I owe you an apology for my earlier comments about your dog. I know it doesn't excuse my actions, but the situation had me on edge, and I allowed my frustration to get the best of me. I have never witnessed a dog like yours perform scent detection work. Most of our patrol dogs are typically German shepherds or Malinois."

The transformation in the sergeant's demeanor was remarkable. He expressed genuine gratitude for Stevie's exceptional performance and hard work. I was overwhelmed with pride, and a smile crept across my face as I shared with the sergeant that Stevie had excelled at detection work and had been blind since birth. The concept of a blind dog being able to thrive in such demanding tasks was initially met with disbelief.

The sergeant chuckled in disbelief, thinking I was joking. "Come on now, you're pulling my leg. A blind dog navigating through the woods while searching for an odor? That's quite a tale!"

Observing our conversation, Amanda said, "Yes, Stevie is indeed blind, just like a bat. But he and Marina make an incredible team, overcoming every obstacle in their path."

I thanked Amanda for her kind words and realized it was the perfect moment to showcase Stevie's abilities and demonstrate his blindness to the police officers. To do so, I decided to prove Stevie's exceptional skills by releasing him off the leash in a secure area and throwing his favorite red squeaky toy. With unwavering determination, Stevie utilized his powerful sense of smell to track down the familiar scent of his beloved toy. His heightened sniffing, increased alertness, and focused attention on the target area became more evident as he got closer to the toy.

The officers and others stood in astonishment as they witnessed Stevie's precision and unwavering commitment, skillfully using his nose to locate the toy despite his blindness. It was a truly extraordinary moment.

Our first assignment proved to be an extraordinary success, showcasing Stevie's remarkable talent and unwavering dedication. The Police Department expressed their gratitude and honored us with a certification of completed work, reinforcing our effectiveness in the field.

After the thorough briefing with Janet and the police officers, I gratefully sank into the car seat, finally able to rest. Fatigue washed over me, as it had been an incredibly long and demanding day. However, as I began to settle in, a peculiar sensation tingled on my legs. Panic surged through me, and I instinctively reached down by my boot, grasping something between my fingers. With a mixture of shock and disgust, I examined it closely, only to let out a piercing scream. "Oh no, ticks are crawling all over my legs!"

Frantically, I scanned my clothes, and to my horror, they were infested with those tiny pests. At that moment, my heart sank as I thought about poor Stevie. I hurriedly checked him, and much to my dismay, he was just as covered in ticks as I was. It seemed like there was no escape from these relentless creatures.

Amanda, overhearing my exclamation, sympathetically informed me that North Carolina was notorious for its abundant tick population. While I had been vaguely aware of this fact, I never expected to encounter such a rampant number of ticks crawling all over us. Understanding our predicament, Amanda kindly offered us a respite at her house, where we could clean ourselves thoroughly.

Once at Amanda's place, I wasted no time. I swiftly shed my infested clothing in the garage, sealing them in a garbage bag. There was no way I was lugging those clothes back to Florida with me. With relief, I stepped into the shower, scrubbing away any lingering ticks and their unwelcome traces. As for Stevie, he received a well-deserved bath, followed by the application of a fast-acting waterproof flea and tick topical to ensure his protection.

That night, we stayed over at Amanda's house, taking the opportunity to celebrate our triumph. We embarked on our journey back home the following day with a renewed sense of accomplishment. Little did I know, I mistakenly believed I had left the ticks behind in North Carolina. As I drove, an itch behind my ear caught my attention, and to my dismay, I discovered another tick attached to my skin. Acting without hesitation, I promptly removed it. Needless to say, I had learned my lesson, and since that day, I have always thoroughly cleaned behind my ears to prevent any unwelcome surprises.

Chapter 10

Trip To Spain

Our departure for Spain felt more charged with excitement than usual, not solely due to the familiar anticipation of our annual summer trip but because this time, we were to be joined by a new travel companion Stevie, who was a little more than two years old. Over the years, my sons and I had woven this pilgrimage into the fabric of our lives, a cherished period when the distraction of everyday life gave way to treasured experiences with loved ones abroad. Stevie's inclusion this year marked a significant milestone; his consistent good behavior in various environments had assured us that he was ready for this larger leap into international travel.

The bustling atmosphere at the airport served as our journey's backdrop as we began to make our way through the crowds, the air vibrant with the sounds of rolling luggage and excited chatter. In such a dynamic environment, I carefully guided Stevie, navigating a path best suited for him. Knowing that dogs are prohibited from escalators, we sought the elevators an easier and safer route for our four-legged friend.

Stevie surprised me with how naturally he adapted to the rhythmic pulse of airport transit. I was reminded of our first elevator ride together as I watched Stevie confidently navigate the elevators.

This moment was a sharp contrast to our earliest experience with elevators. Stevie had been merely a pup back then, and my experience caring for a visually impaired dog was still new. I vividly recall a day when Stevie and I were about to use an elevator together for one of the first times. In the rush of the moment, I made a critical error I turned sharply without signaling to him, failing to communicate the sudden direction change properly. This oversight led to Stevie unwittingly colliding with the elevator's back wall. The sound of the thud filled me with immediate remorse, knowing it resulted from my miscalculation.

However, Stevie's reaction was nothing short of remarkable. Almost immediately, his cheerful spirit shined through as his tail began to wag with that familiar vitality indicative of his forgiving nature and resilient spirit. This small mishap, which could have easily become a source of discouragement, seemed to leave no lasting impression on him. That resilience, that ability to rebound with gleeful innocence, was indicative of his remarkable character a trait that endeared him to us all and reaffirmed my belief that he was, indeed, the perfect addition to our family's Spanish adventures.

In the early stages of Stevie's life, it was imperative for me to use verbal commands to guide him through our daily activities and assist him in understanding his environment. Navigation for Stevie required clear instructions from me, ensuring his safety and comfort as he learned to move in sync with his surroundings.

However, as Stevie grew and our experiences multiplied, a remarkable transformation occurred. The verbal cues I'd once had to provide relentlessly became less necessary. Stevie, through the natural intelligence he possessed and the constancy of routine, began to internalize environmental cues and use them to his advantage. His perception of the world around him evolved, becoming more intuitive and less reliant on my vocal guidance.

Once a symbol of complexity and a challenge for Stevie, elevators gradually became a familiar part of his universe. He came to recognize and anticipate the actions associated with entering and riding one. The progression of steps became a dance that Stevie had mastered with grace and understanding.

The sequence of this routine began with us approaching what, to Stevie, would feel like an abrupt barrier the closed elevator doors. He would stand patiently, his sharp ears picking up the distinct sound of the elevator call button being pressed or the mechanical whisper of the doors sliding open. He learned to discern the subtle change in the atmosphere as the once obstructive barrier gave way to an open passage.

At this cue, we would step forward into the elevator, and here, Stevie displayed his learned sophistication. Knowing that the space was confined, he'd gracefully execute a turn after taking a few steps in, avoiding any risk of an uncomfortable collision with the elevator's interior wall. This maneuver placed him in the perfect spot to stand by my side as we waited for the elevator to encase us again, signaled by the sound of the closing doors. I no longer needed to feed Stevie with a stream of instructions. He had grown to let his other senses take the lead, reading the environment for cues with exceptional adeptness. This silent understanding between Stevie and his world exemplifies the adaptability of animals and demonstrates the deep trust and bond we have developed. For Stevie, the world, with its plethora of sounds, smells, and textures, had become a map he could read with precision, and the journey we took together was a testament to his intelligence and resilience.

In the United States, airlines have specific policies designed to accommodate service dogs to travel with their owners inside the airplane cabin. A typical arrangement allows for the service dog to be positioned at its owner's feet for the duration of the flight.

Thanks to such policies, people like me can have our service dogs stay by our side during air travel. This provision is critical as it spares our service dogs from the stress and potential risks of traveling in the cargo hold, and it spares us from being separated from essential support. The presence of a service dog in the cabin doesn't just offer emotional comfort; it also provides practical assistance and enhances our sense of independence when navigating the complexities of travel.

Before we headed to our departure gate, it was essential to take care of Stevie's needs, given the lengthy flight ahead. I wanted to ensure he was as comfortable as possible and minimize any disruptions that might arise mid-flight.

With our boarding passes in hand, the first order of business was to find a suitable spot for Stevie to relieve himself. After this last bathroom break, our next stop was the security checkpoint. There was a bit of uncertainty on my part regarding the protocols for service dogs like Stevie during the security screening process.

Upon reaching the checkpoint, the TSA agent verified our identification with care and informed me about the procedure. They reassured me that Stevie was permitted to pass through security with me. In the event he set off any alarms, they explained, a secondary check in the form of a pat-down search for both of us would be conducted by an agent to ensure we were not carrying anything prohibited.

With a plan in place, I chose to navigate the security steps methodically. I traversed the metal detector first, leaving Stevie temporarily with my son, Liam. Stevie was visibly unsettled by my temporary absence, pulling on his leash toward me despite Liam's supportive presence.

After successfully passing through the metal detector without any beeps, it was Stevie's turn. I expected his collar and leash, adorned with metal, to trigger the metal detector, so before ushering him through, I crouched down to his level, clapping my hands to signal my proximity and reassure him. He bravely stepped through the metal detector, causing the expected beep.

Upon reaching my side, Stevie couldn't hide his delight, acting as if we had been separated for far longer. I took a moment to soothe his excitement before a TSA agent initiated a gentle pat-down search on Stevie, focusing around his neck and body where the metal was. After a thorough yet careful check, the TSA agent gave us the nod of approval, indicating that security screening was complete and we could proceed to our gate. Our journey continued without further ado.

At Seattle Airport, passengers can take a small train to access different gates. This would be Stevie's inaugural experience with a train, and I was intrigued to see how he might handle this new situation, given he had never been on a train or similar transportation before.

Boarding the train, I found the process pretty straightforward, akin to getting into an elevator, which Stevie had become accustomed to. However, once we settled inside the train and it began its journey, I noticed Stevie became visibly aware of the change. As the train glided along its tracks, he instinctively moved closer to my feet and settled down into a lying position. It was clear that the sensation of the moving train was unfamiliar to him, and he displayed a hint of unease with the rhythm and sway.

Upon our disembarkation, Stevie took a moment to shake off the experience, possibly as a way to alleviate any tension he had felt during the ride. This small action seemed to perk him up, readying him for the next leg of our adventure.

Considering we were facing a lengthy flight, I thought it wise to capitalize on the waiting time available. Taking a leisurely walk around the airport with Stevie would serve us both well. This bit of light exercise was not only a way to keep Stevie at ease but also an opportunity for me to stretch my legs and refresh my mind before embarking on our flight.

When the time came to board the airplane, traveling with a service dog like Stevie offered us the privilege of priority boarding. Once inside the cabin, I showed Stevie the way, knowing he comprehended that my position in front indicated it was time for him to follow. Holding the leash behind me gently ensured that Stevie's head remained lifted as we moved to our seats. My two sons accompanied us, and they helped to ensure that Stevie had ample space on the floor between our seats. Surprisingly, Stevie did not require much space. He cozily nestled into a compact ball at my feet and maintained this position for most of our flight.

Throughout the flight, Stevie was mostly asleep, demonstrating his comfort with the traveling process. Only a couple of instances broke his serenity the moments of takeoff and when the airplane's landing gear was deployed. The significant noise during these times prompted Stevie to seek reassurance by sitting closer to my legs. In response, I offered gentle pats and soothing words, softly telling him, "It's okay, my sweet boy." This seemed to help, as he soon relaxed and slipped back into slumber.

With each journey we've taken, Stevie has grown more familiar with the routine of flying. It's fascinating to observe. As soon as we settle into our seats, Stevie instinctively stretches out and falls asleep, showcasing how attuned he has become to the airplane's rhythms. He senses the cues around him, such as the ding of the seat belt sign, alerting him to when it's acceptable to move about. Watching him navigate these processes so adeptly, from the onset of the flight until we reach the gate at its conclusion, is a testament to his ability to learn and adapt to the intricacies of air travel.

After a long journey through the air for over nine hours, plus the time spent navigating customs and collecting our luggage, we were all ready for a break especially Stevie. Once we arrived in Barcelona and were met with the affectionate embraces of my parents greeting my children, I took it upon myself to attend to Stevie's needs.

Throughout our trip, Stevie maintained his composure and waited patiently for outdoor breaks to take care of his necessities. Indoors, within the airport's confines, he remained calm, trotting beside me with reserved poise. Yet, the moment we moved toward the airport's exit and the scent of open air greeted his senses, I could feel a change. He eagerly pressed forward, tugging the leash slightly a sure sign that nature's call was urgent.

As we stepped outside as if on cue, Stevie lost no time and began to relieve himself. Caught amid the bustle of the airport entrance, I softly but firmly directed a "no" at Stevie, quickly ushering him toward a more appropriate location where he could comfortably and discreetly finish his business. It was abundantly clear that Stevie's discomfort needed to be handled with empathy and haste; it was my duty to ensure that he had a proper place to alleviate himself after the long duration he'd been held.

After a wonderful time soaking in the energy and sights of Barcelona with my father, the moment came to leave the city's hustle and bustle behind. While Stevie appeared to enjoy the city walks, I sensed he was missing the wide-open spaces of nature. With his needs in mind, we planned to take a train to the quaint village of Pardines, set in the heart of Catalunya's Pyrenees. My aunt and uncle, who lived there, kindly offered us a place to stay for the next few weeks.

Upon our arrival at my aunt and uncle's home in Pardines, the warmth of family greeted us. Over the years, they had always welcomed my pets just as they would any family member, and this visit was no exception. However, this particular reunion was buzzing with an extra layer of excitement. My extended family was eager to meet Stevie; they had heard much about his remarkable abilities and looked forward to seeing him in action.

During our stay in Pardines, Stevie was about to be introduced to a completely different environment filled with farm animals. Our gracious neighbors had agreed to let him meet their chickens and lively rabbits, which lived right under the wooden floorboards of their quaint house. All was quiet when we reached the neighbor's barn, where the animals stayed cozy and sheltered. But as soon as we entered the outdoor pen, there was a discernible shift in Stevie's demeanor. The sound of the chickens clucking and the particular scent of the birds captivated him instantly. With his nose on the ground, he eagerly sniffed out the trails of the chickens left in their wake, barely containing his excitement. I had to keep a tight hold on Stevie's leash, shortening it to ensure he didn't indulge too much in the remnants left by the poultry.

Carme, our neighbor, and a friend, deftly let the chickens out for their daily dose of sunlight and fresh air. Stevie was completely attuned to their movements as they made their appearance, his ears standing to attention. Encouraged by Carme's assurance that the chickens were no strangers to dogs, I cautiously let Stevie get a closer look. The chickens themselves seemed to rejoice in the freedom of the open space, unperturbed by our presence.

Stevie took the lead, his nose working overtime, guiding him closer to his new feathered friends. His investigation was thorough, and he was just an inch away when one bold hen strutted right up to him and lightly brushed his face with her feathers. The sensation sparked an immediate reaction from Stevie, who playfully jumped back as if surprised by this close encounter.

After a brief moment of stillness, as if processing the unexpected interaction, Stevie seemed to decide on a new course of action and made a spirited dash toward the chickens. The leash held him back, but it was an endearing sight to see Stevie's pursuit was earnest but harmless. The savvy chickens skillfully dodged every one of Stevie's lighthearted attempts to catch them, always staying one step ahead of his eager paws. We were all entertained by the spectacle filled with laughter and affection for Stevie's harmless and playful conduct.

Pardines is a quaint village that offers peace and charm with its small size and few streets. The village streets are ancient and narrow, without the space for sidewalks, and this leads to very little car traffic, giving Pardines a quiet, serene feeling. These features make it perfect for Stevie to explore without the usual constraints of vehicular disturbance.

From the beginning of our stay, I allowed Stevie the liberty to walk off-leash, feeling confident in the safe environs of the village. To keep our connection strong, I constantly communicated with him through an array of familiar phrases like "I am here,"

"Good boy,"

"Yes," "Right," and "Easy." These cues helped reassure Stevie of my close presence and fostered our bond.

Stevie used his remarkable sense of touch and keen hearing to navigate around the village streets expertly. He cleverly used the walls along the streets, lightly brushing against them with his fur to gauge his location without bumping into them. He could also detect changes in the ground's texture under his paws, using this sense of touch to confirm his whereabouts as he moved.

Whenever Stevie encountered an open space where the touch of the walls was absent, he would pause and wait for my voice to guide him. I would provide the necessary auditory signals, letting him know when to turn or proceed. This consistent and careful approach allowed us to navigate smoothly without any hitches.

Over the course of our first two days in Pardines, as we continued with our routine, Stevie grew more familiar with the village's layout and the positioning of houses. His impressive ability to adjust and understand his surroundings demonstrated his advanced cognitive skills. It seemed as though Stevie had an internal map, allowing him to find his way perhaps even better than an average person might.

The combination of Stevie's sensory skills and our continuous communication led to an inseparable partnership. This special relationship enabled Stevie to explore Pardines confidently and easily, turning the simple village streets into a place of comfort and interest for both Stevie and me.

In the picturesque rural setting of Pardines, where verdant hills roll gently, and farmers tend to their daily routines, a rich tapestry of farm life unfolds, complete with an assortment of livestock that graces the land. Here, the local farmers maintain a diverse collection of animals, among which cows and horses are the most prominent. The setting is serene, with these animals often seen grazing leisurely in the mountainous terrains surrounding the village, embodying the idyllic country life.

Having already experienced the pleasure of mingling with chickens, Stevie was about to broaden his horizons. Before this, he had never encountered such large creatures as cows and horses.

Seizing the opportunity for Stevie to acquaint himself with these larger animals, I decided to venture out to the pastures. These pastures, frequented by the grazing cows, presented the perfect chance for Stevie to observe and interact with bovine creatures in their natural habitat.

With a sense of eagerness and a hint of the unknown, it wasn't long before we set out, journeying to where the cows dotted the landscape like moving parts of the scenic view. This trip was more than just a walk; it was an introduction to the wider world of farm life for Stevie and an expansion of his animal compendium. The experience promised to endow him with a new level of understanding and appreciation for the creatures that share our world. I was intent on making this introduction as soon as possible.

As the car drew nearer to the pastoral expanse where the livestock grazed, I made sure to park as close as possible to provide Stevie with the opportunity for an up-close encounter with the grazing farm animals. Leaving the confines of the vehicle behind, we stepped out into the open, and immediately, Stevie's senses were inundated with the unfamiliar yet fascinating smells of the countryside.

The crisp mountain air, filled with myriad new scents, was thrilling for Stevie, who began investigating the area with his nose twitching in excitement. After assessing the surroundings and feeling confident in the environment's safety, I decided to give Stevie more liberty to satisfy his curiosity by letting him off his leash. Stevie darted off energetically with newfound freedom, his nose nearly scraping the grass as he tracked the smells that danced through the breeze. His path may have seemed random and unstructured to the casual observer, but his canine instincts were finely tuned. Unbeknownst to me, Stevie was on a mission, lured by horse manure's pungent yet appealing scent.

When I realized what Stevie was so fervently tracking, panic momentarily set in such material could be harmful if he ingested it or rolled in it. Reacting quickly, I started to hasten toward him, focusing on intercepting his goal. My voice carried firmly over the distance and a command meant to halt his quest: "Leave it!"

Stevie responded to my directive with unexpected immediacy to my relief and admiration. Although his natural urges tempted him to persist, my consistent command and gentle but firm corrections redirected his behavior. The lesson took repeated attempts, but Stevie's focus gradually shifted, and his interest in the horse droppings faded. With continued guidance and reinforcement, he soon ignored them, turning his attention to the other wonders the pasture had to offer.

Our journey continued, meandering through the tranquil countryside until we arrived at a pastoral scene where cows and horses were peacefully grazing. As we neared these pastoral giants, I observed a distinct change in Stevie's demeanor. His previously brisk trot slowed to a deliberate, careful pace. His body lowered toward the earth, belly almost brushing against the grass, moving with a stealth usually reserved for stalking. It was evident that Stevie was acutely aware of the farm animals' presence, potentially picking up on their unique scents wafting through the air, the subtle tremors of their movement resonating through the ground, and the soft symphony of their sounds in the distance.

The cows displayed a typical disinterest, barely acknowledging our arrival before deciding to distance themselves with a casual saunter. Conversely, the horses exhibited a contrasting curiosity, particularly drawn to Stevie's unusual approach. As Stevie advanced, his movements became even more calculated and reserved until he finally positioned himself flat on the ground with only his head held up in alertness; it looked like his eyes were fixed upon the equine creatures. It was as if the horses were seeing a creature like Stevie for the first time, their attention fully fixated on him.

During this moment of silent communication, a foal emerged as notably inquisitive among the herd. With a slow, cautious gait that mirrored a delicate dance, the foal edged closer to Stevie, who remained motionless, his head locked on the approaching figure. He seemed to be analyzing the foal's scent and presence, trying to understand this new encounter.

Their noses brushed ever so slightly in a tender moment of interspecies greeting. This tactile interaction, reminiscent of Stevie's earlier encounter with chickens, prompted an immediate and exaggerated leap from him. Both animals seemed equally startled by the connection, resulting in a pause filled with surprise for the foal, Stevie, and myself.

But the encounter was far from over. Recovering from their initial shock, the foal, showing a youthful boldness, ventured toward Stevie again. This time, however, Stevie stood erect, his posture more confident, engaging in another bout of olfactory investigation with the foal. While Stevie's precise thoughts escaped my understanding, his body language suggested a desire to play. He emitted a playful bark and a bow typical of a playful invitation, signaling his friendly intentions. Still adjusting to Stevie's canine etiquette, the foal seemed intrigued yet puzzled by this display of playful advances.

Over the next few minutes, an astonishing exchange unfolded before my eyes. Both Stevie and the foal continued to interact, sniffing and observing each other, a mutual fascination growing between them. Witnessing such an interaction, seemingly cross-species communication evolving into a playful bond, was magical. The delightful scene served as a gentle reminder of life's simple, joyous moments, transcending the barriers of species and language.

I could sense Stevie's weariness as we returned to the car after our outing. He plodded along right beside me, his pace slowing down with every step. Despite his evident exhaustion, Stevie's instincts remained sharp, especially when it came to scents that would delight any dog's olfactory sense. To him, the robust odor of cow dung was an irresistible perfume, drawing him in with an almost magnetic pull.

In an instant, Stevie stumbled upon a sizable cow patty, and without my immediate realization, he indulged in his primal canine desire. He dived into the manure, dropping, swirling, and rolling with abandon. It was as if he reasoned, "If I'm not meant to eat this, the next best thing is to anoint myself in its essence!" And that's precisely what Stevie did. His enthusiasm for his earthy bath was uncontainable, as he kept at it until every inch of his coat was adorned with the farm-fresh manure.

At that moment, looking at Stevie, I saw the epitome of canine joy. His movements were expressive it was as if every part of him was laughing and smiling in the language of a dog. The sight of Stevie in such rapture made any thoughts of annoyance dissipate. Instead, I laughed alongside him, sharing his peculiar revelry.

Our fortune turned as we came across a small, meandering creek a stroke of luck in the messy aftermath of Stevie's adventure. There, I took the opportunity to wash away the layers of manure. While it wasn't a thorough cleaning, I did manage to remove enough of the muck to make Stevie presentable for the car ride home. It was a hasty and imperfect cleanup, but it was the best I could do under the circumstances.

We drove back to Pardines with the windows down to let in the fresh air. Despite having washed Stevie in the creek, the pungent odor of cow manure lingered stubbornly. Stevie, unaffected by the smell, settled down as soon as the car began to move. He quickly drifted off to sleep, resting so peacefully that he seemed to be smiling in his slumber. It was clear that the day's adventures had worn him out, allowing him to sleep contentedly like a child, undisturbed by the remaining scent.

After our stay in Pardines, we traveled to Port de la Selva, a slightly larger village located on the Catalonian coast known as La Costa Brava. The setting in Port de la Selva contrasted with the tranquil, traffic-free environment of Pardines due to its busier streets filled with tourists and more frequent vehicular activity. Consequently, I could not give Stevie the same level of freedom he had enjoyed previously; it was necessary to keep him on a leash for his safety and to be considerate of the public.

We arrived at the beach as the Mediterranean sun cast its warm glow over the coastline. Even during our visits to the bustling beaches, I had to ensure Stevie remained on a short leash. His excitement about the proximity to the water was palpable, but unlike our experiences on the more private shores of Florida, I had to be cautious here. The freedom to run unrestrained had to be curtailed to avoid any disturbances.

Stevie didn't seem to mind the leash; his spirits remained high despite the restraint. I walked him close to the water's edge, carefully navigating through the throngs of beachgoers. Stevie moved beside me, and I was vigilant to prevent him from accidentally stepping on any sunbathers. The beach was dotted with people reclining and enjoying the sun, which made it quite a task to find a path through the sea of individuals without causing any disruption. It was indeed challenging to ensure both Stevie's enjoyment and the undisturbed relaxation of the people around us.

I sought out a more private area along the water's edge for recreation. Fortunately, we discovered the perfect spot away from the busy main stretches where the sea formed a shallow basin, the waters reaching just below my knees. It was the ideal depth for a fun splash with Stevie.

The moment Stevie's paws met the gentle embrace of the sea, his demeanor transformed. His tail wagging with delight, he gleefully pranced through the crystal-clear shallows, sending ripples dancing across the surface. Seizing the moment, I selected a toy from our beach bag, one he had grown particularly fond of, and tossed it a modest distance into the water. Stevie's ears perked with acute attentiveness, tuning in to the subtle splash that marked the entry point of his adored plaything. Yet, as the toy hit the water, it betrayed expectations and quickly disappeared beneath the surface.

Anxiety gripped me momentarily as Stevie paddled eagerly toward where the toy had vanished. I held my breath, half-expecting him to lose interest or become too tired to persist in his aquatic quest. But Stevie's spirits were undeterred; his determination was staunch, bolstered by a steadfast belief that his cherished toy was waiting to be retrieved from the depths.

Stevie's pace became meticulous as he neared the targeted area; each stroke of his paws was calculated. His nostrils flared as he inhaled deeply, discerning the scents on the water, which could guide him to his submerged prize. Suddenly, with a determined plunge, Stevie submerged his head under the water's surface, his furry ears momentarily disappearing into the blue. One ... two attempts, and then on the third, his head resurfaced, this time with the toy securely gripped in his teeth. The sight was joyous; with his goal achieved, Stevie paddled back to shore, exuding the unmistakable air of a victorious retriever, eager for the next round.

However, with the beach's population growing as more people arrived to enjoy the sun, sand, and surf, I felt it was best to conclude our game to avoid disturbing the peaceful harmony of the beachgoers. I headed to our beach setup to fetch Stevie some fresh drinking water. Engrossed in this task, the leash slipped from my grasp, unnoticed.

When my son's quiet prompt drew my gaze, I spotted Stevie expertly weaving his way through the expanding tapestry of beach towels and sunbathers. His movements were gentle and assured; he didn't impose upon a single person's space as he trod the sandy terrain. About forty feet from our spot, he found what he was instinctually searching for a bowl filled with fresh, clean water courtesy of another dog-loving family. Stevie's urgent thirst took precedence, and he didn't hesitate to gracefully help himself.

Watching Stevie employ such finesse and intelligence to distinguish between the rough textures of the beach and the soft fibers of the towels to navigate the crowded space truly astounded me. This revelation perfectly highlighted his remarkable sensory perception feeling the subtle differences enabled him to tread carefully, avoiding disturbing the beachgoers to find his destination. It was a testament to Stevie's innate ability to make sense of his world with precision and care.

The journey through Spain had been a treasure trove of experiences, delighting each member of our traveling party and opening up a world of adventure for Stevie. As the days swept by, the conclusion of our Spanish escapade approached. But the end of one journey marked the beginning of another; we were not bound for our previous home in

Florida. Instead, we were destined for a new chapter on the sun-drenched shores of St. Croix in the Virgin Islands.

Our relocation to St. Croix was sparked by a significant career opportunity for my husband when he was offered a position as a port captain. This professional shift came at an opportune moment as we contemplated a change that would enhance our family dynamics.

Before the move, Joe's career as a ship's captain demanded extensive periods at sea. His voyages often spanned several months, creating a recurring absence felt deeply within our household. During these intervals, I shouldered the responsibilities of parenting alone, caring for our two young sons, Sean, aged seven, and Liam, aged five. The prolonged separations were challenging for the entire family, particularly as they precluded Joe from witnessing our boys' developmental milestones and everyday achievements firsthand.

Moreover, the boys were acutely feeling the void left by their father a father figure's presence is keenly significant during such formative years. The physical distance between Joe and our sons hampered the nurturing those irreplaceable paternal bonds.

With the acceptance of this new role in the U.S. Virgin Islands, a stark contrast to his previous position was promised. Joe would no longer be bound to lengthy sojourns at sea, and the job would enable him to come home to us every day. This change meant no more travel for him, which we anticipated would strengthen our family unit. The chance to have daily interaction and shared experiences signified an invaluable improvement to our lives, offering both Joe and our sons the opportunity to make up for lost time and develop a stronger, more engaged familial connection.

Anticipation hung in the air as we prepared to make the transition from the well-trodden cobbled streets and breezy mountaintops of Spain to the tropical allure of St. Croix. This idyllic island promised to deliver a distinctive Caribbean adventure, brimming with verdant landscapes and azure waters, a stark and exhilarating contrast to the places Stevie had come to know.

For Stevie especially, St. Croix was an entire canvas of uncharted experiences waiting to unfold. Picturing him exploring the lush terrain with its unique aromas, listening to the rhythm of the waves, and feeling the warmth of the powdery sand beneath his paws was heartening. The move harbored the potential for growth and discovery for Stevie and all of us as we braced ourselves to embrace the unknown with the fresh perspective that comes with a new environment.

St. Croix beckoned with promises of exploration and learning, from the grooves of its historical towns to the rich, untamed rainforests and the vibrant underwater tapestry coral reefs present. Our family was ready to forge new memories, adapt to new surroundings, and immerse ourselves in island life's carefree yet vibrant spirit. Indeed, it was not just a new home but a new opportunity for adventure in the alluring tropics, an untouched territory awaiting our footprints.

Chapter 11

Moving To St. Croix

Our journey to St. Croix spanned a wearying two days of travel from our previous visit to Spain. Despite the weariness, our spirits were lifted by the prospect of beginning anew in the tropical glamour of St. Croix, a gem among the U.S. Virgin Islands. Upon arrival and a brief period of acclimatization within the confines of our new rental home still strewn with unopened boxes my husband suggested that a trip to the beach might be the perfect way to immerse ourselves in the island's splendor.

The need to unwind was paramount, especially for Stevie. The move had undoubtedly been disruptive for him after more than forty hours in transit and a direct transfer from the hustle of the airport to the chaos of our unsettled house, confusion and a sense of disorientation would be natural for any dog. The beach promised an open sanctuary where Stevie could release his pent-up energy and regain his bearings.

The beach we chose was picturesque, graced with powdery white sands, set against the backdrop of luminous turquoise waters, and bordered by vibrant greenery. Palm trees danced to the rhythm of the soft ocean breeze, providing a sanctuary of cool shade amid the tropical heat. The enticing, warm waters beckoned for a tranquil swim, an adventurous snorkeling session, and the discovery of the colorful local sea life.

Given the beach's ample space, it was far from crowded, offering our family and Stevie a sense of solitude and freedom. While Stevie indulged in joyful sprints along the shoreline and swam in the welcoming embrace of the sea, we had the luxury of basking under the sun or delving beneath the water's surface to snorkel. This serene coastal haven proved to be an idyllic setting for all of us to relax and adjust to our new life in this beautiful island paradise.

Having enjoyed a rejuvenating time at the beach, my husband and I turned our attention to transforming the chaos of our new home into a navigable and secure environment for Stevie. Our first task was to clear and define pathways amid the clutter of moving boxes. We meticulously stacked the boxes, ensuring each pile was stable and eliminating any risk of them toppling onto Stevie or our young sons, Sean and Liam.

We measured the pathways' width using Stevie's body length as a guide, allowing him enough room to pass freely and comfortably without brushing against the boxes. Any boxes with sharp corners or jutting edges were quickly addressed we wrapped them with towels or padded them with bubble wrap to soften any inadvertent contact and to prevent potential injuries.

We placed rugs and mats within these pathways to assist Stevie in his orientation, contrasting the floor's textures. These tactile cues would act as signals for Stevie, helping him to differentiate between "safe" areas where he could walk and "off-limits" spaces where the boxes were stored. While we were busy with these preparations, we ensured Stevie was comfortably resting in his crate, safely out of harm's way, and catching up on sleep.

Once the pathways were secure and the preventive measures were in place, I carefully led Stevie out of his crate. Gently guiding him along the newly created walkways, we repeated this process several times to help him grow accustomed to his surroundings until he seemed confident enough to navigate them independently. Familiar with adapting to new spaces, Stevie quickly began mentally mapping the layout without needing assistance.

I then addressed our sons with a clear and gentle reminder: "Sean and Liam, we need to keep the boxes and pathways just like this until we've unpacked everything and can remove them. This consistency is important our new home must be a safe space for Stevie and all of us as we settle in." Our collaborative efforts ensured that our home was organized and a sanctuary for the entire family, including our sweet Stevie.

To go out to the backyard of our new home, we were graced with a pair of stunning glass doors that brought elegance to our living area. As we settled into our new abode, I encountered an unexpected yet fascinating happening. My dogs, seemingly unaware of the glass doors' actual position, would occasionally charge headlong into the transparent barriers. They were utterly convinced that the way was clear, a belief that painted a humorous and worrisome picture. It quickly became apparent that we needed to find a remedy for this potentially hazardous confusion.

Amid these gentle collisions, Stevie, a dog who navigated the world from an exceptional vantage point. Blinded from birth, Stevie exercised an extraordinary knack for discerning the presence of the barrier. Lacking sight, he instead relied on the subtle shifts of airflow and the nuances of his environment to inform him. He had an intuitive grace, a sixth sense, that enabled him to detect without fail whether the pathway was open or closed, thereby avoiding the mishaps that occurred to his housemates.

With a remarkable, almost tactile awareness, Stevie moved effortlessly, avoiding the glass obstacles that seemed to challenge his sighted peers.

His heightened other senses appeared to allow him to "see" in a way that compensated for the visual cues he lacked.

Concerned for the well-being of my sighted dogs, who were susceptible to these glass doors' illusion of openness, I implemented a preventive strategy. We affixed stickers to the glass at strategic points, creating visual markers that served as cues to our pets about the true status of the doors. These stickers aimed to prevent further accidental run-ins by clearly indicating the doors when they were closed.

Stevie, in his unique adaptability, remained blissfully indifferent to these visual aids. His impressive, inherent ability to sense his surroundings meant he had no use for such indicators. He navigated with confidence, his inherent perception of the world guiding him flawlessly through open and closed doors. His success stood as a testament to the incredible capabilities of animals to adapt and thrive, regardless of their physical limitations.

A week had passed since we'd settled into our new home on St. Croix, with everything in its rightful place, when the day arrived for Sean and Liam to start their new school adventure. Living off the main bus route, I drove them to school each morning, and on that first day, I accompanied Liam to his first-grade classroom. The new environment was overwhelming for him, so I stayed by his side for reassurance.

As was our custom, Stevie joined us. Beaming with pride, Liam held Stevie's leash and eagerly shared with anyone who would listen that his dog was blind, showing off Stevie with a sense of awe and affection.

One morning after the school drop-off, I was approached by a friendly face who introduced herself as Marta. "Hi, I am Marta, and my son is in your son's class," she said. Curiosity soon followed as Marta inquired about Stevie, marveling at his calm demeanor and the level of his training. During our conversation, I shared that we were new to the island and mentioned my dual skills as a dog trainer and a veterinary technician.

Her expression lit up as she relayed an opportunity: "Just what my father is looking for. My father owns an animal clinic here and needs a veterinary technician. You could bring your résumé to the clinic, or I could pass it along to him for you."

Excited about the prospect, I immediately expressed my interest and arranged to provide Marta with my résumé that afternoon during school pick-up, where I would also get to meet her father in person.

Come afternoon, on the school playground, I was introduced to Dr. Paul Hess, Marta's father. As the boys lost themselves in play, Dr. Hess and I chatted warmly for ten minutes. His compassionate character was readily apparent, and he extended an invitation for me to visit his clinic the following day to see if the environment and team were a good fit for me, with the possibility of beginning work immediately.

That next day marked the initiation of my tenure at the Island Animal Clinic. As I stepped through the doors, a wave of positive energy welcomed me. The staff was genuinely friendly toward both Stevie and me, who had quickly been accommodated with a secure spot to rest during my shifts. Dr. Hess and I felt an instant rapport.

Within the nurturing environment of the Island Animal Clinic, I was introduced to Dr. Michelle, an accomplished veterinarian who also lent her expertise to the nearby St. Croix Animal Welfare Center. It was serendipitous that the Welfare Center was currently in search of a part-time veterinary technician to fill a role that required availability for two days a week.

Given that my schedule at the Island Animal Clinic was also part-time, the opportunity at the Welfare Center aligned perfectly with my availability, presenting a chance to broaden my professional horizons. I embraced the idea wholeheartedly and decided to extend my services to the shelter as well.

Assuming responsibilities at both the Island Animal Clinic and the St. Croix Animal Welfare Center allowed me to fully engage with my vocation as a veterinary technician. These dual roles deepened my engagement with animal care, enabling me to contribute to the well-being of numerous animals and their human companions on the island. My work nurtured my passion for veterinary medicine. It allowed me to become an integral part of the close-knit island community, forming bonds through the shared love and care for animals.

I allocated most of my working hours to the animal shelter, recognizing that my assistance was valuable there. Accompanying me daily was Stevie, who rapidly grew accustomed to and was warmly welcomed at the shelter. His presence became well-known among the animals and the staff, with his enthusiastic tail wags greeting everyone. For Stevie, the shelter offered a myriad of new and intriguing sensory experiences, from the distinct sounds and smells to the array of visual cues that he, despite his blindness, could perceive and explore an enriching contrast to our earlier environment.

During Stevie's first days at the animal shelter, the atmosphere was intense and new to him. He was immediately met with an offensive of sounds, primarily due to the incessant barking from various dogs. This, coupled with the shelter's distinct mix of odors, filled the air and provided a sensory experience different from what he was used to. Initially, this sensory overload seemed to overwhelm Stevie, who was unaccustomed to such a vibrant display of canine conversation and the unique smells of a shared animal environment.

As time passed, Stevie began to adapt to the crowded shelter environment. Observing this adjustment, I decided it was a good time to introduce him to the other dogs at the facility more closely. It soon became apparent that Stevie had a unique approach to engaging with his fellow canines. Intriguingly, he was drawn to the dogs with the loudest barks. The size was no object to him; the volume piqued his interest. He seemed to use their loud barks as auditory landmarks, navigating the shelter grounds by ear, as if the resounding barks acted like sonar pings guiding a ship through fog.

Stevie's playful nature didn't take long to manifest. In a humorous and heartwarming spectacle, he would often join in the choir of barking dogs, his voice joining the symphony with unrestrained zest. He'd do this while maintaining a firm grip on one of his cherished toys, often a ball, seemingly convinced that his barks would help him stand out in the canine crowd. As he added his voice to the mix, he'd trot around in joyous loops, the ball still secured in his mouth.

It was clear that Stevie believed his bark would help others pinpoint his location, completely unaware that his four-legged peers had no trouble seeing him without vocal assistance. This misunderstanding only added to the charm of the spectacle. Watching Stevie joyfully bark with his toys clamped between his teeth was truly heartwarming. Each bark, muffled by the ball, resonated with a contagious joy and vivacity. It was a simple, pure display of canine bliss that never failed to bring a smile to my face, reminding me to appreciate the small joys and the playful spirit of my delightful furry friend.

Our workdays at the animal shelter revolved around a small yet welcoming space that served as my operations hub. Here, I meticulously carried out all the necessary preparations before each animal underwent surgery a crucial step in ensuring the seamless flow of spaying and neutering operations spearheaded by the skilled veterinarian.

Right there, beside me, within this comforting enclosure, was Stevie's designated area. He had a plush bed, thoughtfully placed by the window, that allowed him to bask in the gentle rays of sunlight.

The room's ambiance was primarily defined by my scent mingling within, creating an environment unmistakably familiar to Stevie. This sense of familiarity was his anchor, instilling a feeling of safety amid the clinic's daily din. Nevertheless, the regular sound of the clinic's door creaking open and then shut would occasionally stir him. Amid these auditory interruptions, a flicker of concern regarding my presence might surface within him.

Compelled by a mix of anxiety and curiosity, Stevie would stir himself from his cozy nook. Weaving through the room with an elegant poise that belied his internal unease, he'd embark on his short journey to track me down. His quest would end with the soft nudge of his nose against my skin his loving gesture conveying relief and affection.

Each time he sought me out and found me, my silent promises of companionship and protection seemed to fill him with peace. Comforted by the confirmation of my presence, Stevie would gladly retreat to his bed, lulled into a serene slumber by the knowledge that I was never far away.

These frequent, touching exchanges heightened my awareness of our profound connection. In those moments, I would offer him more than just my proximity; I'd provide verbal solace, easing any lingering trepidation. With a gentle tone, I'd reassure him with simple, heartfelt phrases like "Stevie, my sweet boy, I am here" words that bridged any physical distance between us with the power of sound and emotion. This ritual of reassurance strengthened the trust between us, reinforcing Stevie's sense of security and my role as his steadfast guardian within the bustling world of the shelter veterinary clinic.

In my role at the animal welfare center, we commonly received an influx of young animals, particularly kittens and puppies. These creatures often required temporary foster care, as they were too young to stay at the shelter or to be immediately placed up for adoption. During my introductory week at the center, I was taken by the idea of offering my home as a

nurturing haven for such animals. I thought fostering kittens would provide a delightful and educational experience for my sons, Liam and Sean, allowing them to learn about caregiving responsibilities.

One of my colleagues kindly agreed to transport the kittens a pair of four-week-old balls of fur directly to our home. Meanwhile, I was intrigued by the prospect of introducing Stevie to these new additions;

as far as I could remember, he hadn't encountered kittens before.

Upon returning home with Stevie after our day at the center, we were greeted by scenes of instant camaraderie. Sean and Liam were fully engaged, reveling in the joy of interacting with the tiny feline duo. The kittens quickly became the focus of attention, capturing the hearts of the boys with their playful antics and endearing vulnerability.

As was his routine, Stevie confidently entered the house and navigated his familiar surroundings easily, relying on his memory of the layout rather than his sense of sight. Suddenly, a new scent caught his attention. The foster kittens, charcoal and gold tabbies with wide eyes, had ventured into Stevie's space, unsure of their reception.

Stevie paused, his nose twitching, ears perked to catch the soft sound of their paws on the floor. Knowing the kittens had likely never encountered a dog, they remained still, except for their whiskers quivering and tails swaying slowly. The air filled with anticipation.

With cautious steps, Stevie approached, following the scent of the kittens, which carried the fragrance of curious youth and the faint traces of their recent meal. The scent formed a clear image in Stevie's mind, one he understood.

Stevie let out a soft woof, his tail wagging hesitantly as if extending an olive branch. One of the kittens meowed, and they cautiously drew closer. Stevie playfully bowed, then lay down a gentle giant compared to the tiny felines and lowered his head slightly. He moved slowly, aware of his size and unfamiliarity with these situations. The kittens sensed his vulnerability and became absorbed in the unfolding encounter.

The charcoal kitten approached first, gently touching Stevie's paw with its small, wet nose. Stevie's nose worked overtime, capturing every nuance of their presence. They smelled like adventure, like something precious and new. The other kitten followed, brushing its fluffy tail against Stevie's nose, emitting a soft purring vibration. Startled by the unexpected sensation, Stevie jumped up briefly but remained curious about the kittens. He lay down again, and the kittens approached once more. Stevie felt the kittens' purring as they gently kneaded his fur, and he began to lick them. Stevie had gained two new friends.

While driving to the animal welfare one day, I noticed a construction site with a sign declaring "St. Croix Rescue." My curiosity was piqued, so I decided to stop by to learn more about it. I discovered that the St. Croix Rescue Squad provides critical emergency services to the U.S. Virgin Islands community, including medical care and various rescue operations. With nearly a quarter-century of experience, this volunteer-based organization operates 24/7, handling medical emergencies, fire incidents, and land or sea rescues. In addition to their emergency response roles, they offer comprehensive training programs through the St. Croix Rescue Academy for individuals who wish to become skilled volunteers in emergency response. Their Domestic Training Section Office of EMS Education provides emergency response training to public and private sectors of communities under the jurisdiction of the United States. It offers First Aid, CPR, Medical First Responder (MFR), Emergency Medical Technician (EMT), Basic Trauma Life Support (BTLS), Community Emergency Response Team (CERT), Weapons of Mass Destruction (WMD), Mass Casualty Management, and Search and Rescue courses. Also, it is a primary provider of continuing education courses for emergency medical technicians, registered nurses, and physicians.

Upon discovering the St. Croix Rescue organization, I immediately felt a connection and knew it was the search and rescue group I wanted to be part of. While I hadn't extensively researched Search and Rescue (SAR) organizations during the period of our move to the island, I had a clear intention. If the island hosted an SAR, I would like to join.

With this goal in mind, one of the pivotal steps I had taken involved ensuring that my dogs, Aki and Stevie, were certified search-and-rescue K9s. Each had their specialization: Stevie was adept at locating human remains, while Aki was trained in man trailing. Man trailing is an advanced and crucial tracking technique that involves locating specific people by following their unique scent trail. This capability is essential for search-and-rescue operations and valuable in supporting law enforcement during investigations.

When I met with the lieutenant of the St. Croix Rescue team, his enthusiasm about our arrival was unmistakable. He had been eager to add K9 capabilities to their search-and-rescue efforts for some time, and with our arrival, they now had access to experienced and certified K9 units.

Despite the lieutenant's warm reception, the broader team's response was mixed. I sensed a palpable hesitation from the rest of the members toward us. I interpreted their reservation as being twofold: the integration of dogs into their operations and my presence as a white woman in their close-knit community. I understood that as someone new to the area and unfamiliar with local culture and practices, my eagerness to join the team might have been perceived as overstepping.

Moreover, concerns specifically revolved around Aki, my large German shepherd. There was a misconception among some team members who conflated Aki's breed with the stereotypical aggressive police K9s they may have encountered rather than recognizing him as the well-trained search-and-rescue dog he was.

I embarked on a comprehensive training journey to become a part of the St. Croix Rescue team officially. This involved obtaining certification as a Medical First Responder (MFR) along with completing an assortment of search-and-rescue courses pertinent to the responsibilities I would be undertaking.

The training, which spanned four exhaustive months, encompassed in-depth medical instruction and practical outdoor search-and-rescue exercises. Throughout this intense period, Stevie and Aki were my steadfast companions. Their presence provided moral support and served as a living testament to the skills and dedication I brought to the team's mission.

Aki, with his disciplined demeanor, and Stevie, a blind dog who rose above his limitations, both played their part in breaking down initial reservations held by the team. Stevie, in particular, had a profound impact; the fact that he could overcome his visual impairment and still excel in his role resonated with the team. It served to dismantle any lingering skepticism and showcased the boundless potential when overcoming perceived obstacles.

As the team observed the interactions between the dogs and me our communication, mutual respect, and the thoroughness of our training they began to glean insights into my character and aspirations. They recognized my commitment to search and rescue and the well-being of the island's community as a whole. They bore witness to Stevie's amiable nature and Aki's precision, which helped to reshape any prior notion they might have had about them.

With time, the initial uncertainty that shrouded my entry into the team evaporated, morphing into respect and admiration. Stevie, with his inspiring adaptability, and Aki, with his focused expertise, were fully embraced as part of the rescue family. No longer an outsider, I was accepted as a trusted and capable member of the St. Croix Rescue team, ready to utilize our collective skills in serving and protecting the community we were now proud to be a part of.

To meet the physical demands of working with St. Croix Rescue, it was necessary for me to maintain a high level of fitness. Consequently, I took to swimming in the pool at the school my boys attended, often under the warm glow of the island sun. During these swim sessions, a touching scene would often unfold: Stevie, my faithful dog, would position himself right by the edge of the pool. With his tail wagging in a gentle rhythm, mirroring the splash of the water, he would lie down and face toward me, his attention fixed as I swam back and forth in the clear blue water. His devoted presence was a comforting constant as I exercised.

As I submerged myself in the cool, refreshing waters, the energy of my lap reverberated through the air, creating an atmosphere charged with excitement. Stevie, sensitive to the vibrations rippling through the water, sensed a symphony in each of my strokes. Even though his sight was veiled in darkness, he became a master at deciphering the movements, using his other senses as a compass to guide him toward my location in the pool.

With each graceful lap completed, Stevie's enthusiasm grew. His wet nose quivered with anticipation, detecting the faintest scent emanating from the water's surface. His ears perked up, attuned to the soft ripples and lively splashes, painting a vivid tapestry of motion in his imaginative mind.

What fascinated me was Stevie's undeniable love for swimming in pools. Whenever we visited someone with a pool, Stevie's excitement was palpable. He would eagerly approach the pool, his nose catching the scent of the water. With deliberate steps, he would walk around the edge of the pool, meticulously mapping it in his mind. This ritual seemed to be his way of familiarizing himself with his aquatic playground.

Then, without hesitation, Stevie would take the plunge. He would gracefully leap into the water, his body gliding through the shimmering surface. A few leisurely laps around the pool would follow as if he were savoring every moment of the cool water against his fur. And when he had his fill, Stevie would calmly find his way back to the edge, flawlessly navigating his return path.

The method of exiting the pool seemed to be of no concern to Stevie. He would always find the edge of the pool and follow it to the way out. Whether it was a set of large steps or a pool ladder, he instinctively knew that either way would lead him back to dry land. However, there was one pool that Stevie recognized as off-limits the boys' school pool.

Despite his fondness for swimming, he never attempted to jump into that particular pool. It led me to speculate that Stevie could discern the distinction between pools based on the sounds of splashing and the more pungent scent of chlorine.

Stevie's ability to differentiate between pools, his eagerness to explore, and his understanding of boundaries truly fascinated me. It emphasized his deep connection with the world of swimming and left me in awe of his sensory perception and intuitive understanding of his surroundings.

Living on St. Croix, my sons and I engaged in various enriching activities, including participating in the local chapter of the Boy Scouts. Sean and Liam were proud members of the St. Croix Boy Scouts, an organization strongly emphasizing nurturing wilderness skills, promoting community service, and building a sense of brotherhood among its young members.

The Boy Scouts on the island boasted their own campsite, a natural haven that we had the joy of utilizing for multiple camping trips. These outings were not only adventures in the great outdoors but were also key opportunities for Sean and Liam to develop essential survival skills and bond with their fellow Scouts.

Stevie, who had always been a part of our family's excursions, was enthusiastically welcomed on these camping trips. Everyone was celebrating his attendance; both children and adults were charmed by his gentle nature and ability to navigate the campsite despite his blindness. His presence became an enduring part of our adventures, and he was just as much a member of the Scout community as any of the boys. Each time we set out for a camping adventure with the Scout troop, Stevie was our beloved companion, adding to the warmth and fellowship of these communal experiences.

During one particular camping trip, an inquisitive Eagle Scout approached me with a request: he was curious if Stevie and I could demonstrate Stevie's detection talents. It was an opportunity I embraced with enthusiasm but with an intention to add an educative twist.

Upon arrival at the camp, a minor incident occurred: one of the children suffered a nosebleed, resulting in his T-shirt being stained with blood. It was my practice to collect such items in a sealed gallon ziplock bag to later serve as training materials for Stevie. However, in this case, the bloodied shirt would become a central prop in our impending demonstration for the Scouts.

As the demonstration commenced, I took a moment to explain the function and significance of a human remain detection K9, emphasizing how such skills are applied in real-life scenarios. I shared captivating stories of past deployments, including the first mission where Stevie successfully tracked down an injured individual, holding the Scouts' attention.

As I was narrating Stevie's past exploits to the intrigued boys, a volunteer one of Sean's friends quietly slipped away to assist with our demonstration. The boy wasn't injured but agreed to simulate being so. He concealed himself with the blood-soaked T-shirt of course, not wearing it but having it handy to add authenticity to the scene. To spice up the demonstration, two other boys also hid nearby, acting as decoys. They lay in wait for about thirty minutes before we began our search.

Before initiating the search, I briefed the boys on a necessary protocol change: I would switch Stevie's everyday service dog vest to a search-and-rescue harness, signaling to him that it was time to embark on a mission. I instructed the Scouts to follow behind us at a safe distance to avoid interfering with Stevie's meticulous search work.

The boys' excitement was tangible and perhaps matched only by Stevie's eager anticipation. As Stevie began his search, I acted as a commentator for the Scouts, explaining each of Stevie's moves. Stevie initially approached a decoy but promptly moved on, an action that left the boys in awe of his discernment.

As we neared the "injured" boy's location, despite the visual cues being evident to us, for Stevie, it was the scent that would guide him. I let Stevie off his lead and instructed the Scouts to halt and observe. Stevie tackled the more challenging route through dense bushes, guided by his acute sense of smell, as I explained to the curious onlookers why he chose: a breeze carrying the blood scent was stronger there, and Stevie, using air scenting techniques, was keenly investigating.

As Stevie insisted on making his way through the thick brush, a sign that he was on the right track, I stepped in to assist him. I reattached him to a long line and guided him around to a narrow path by the mangroves while the boys watched our coordinated efforts from a distance.

Stevie tugged back at first, reluctant to leave the strong scent behind, but as we approached the source on the other side, his tail wagged faster a sure indication of his proximity to the target. As we watched, one of the boys remarked on Stevie's mounting excitement, and I praised the keen observation.

Stevie's zigzagging intensified as he pursued what we termed the "scent cone" the pattern formed by dispersing odor molecules emanating from the hidden boy with the bloodied shirt. I explained this concept to the Scouts, who quietly observed Stevie's methodical approach.

Upon closing to a mere six feet from the boy, Stevie crawled until he reached the boy and the shirt. True to his training, Stevie didn't celebrate just yet; he continued to search until he found the precise source the bloody T-shirt and then calmly lay down beside it, signaling his definitive find.

A Scout posed a thoughtful question about why Stevie did not conclude his search upon first finding the boy. I clarified that Stevie's training focused on locating the scent of blood, not the individual, so the earlier decoys did not distract him.

Impressed and entertained, the boys cheered and applauded Stevie's demonstration, a reaction that, while bewildering to him, stirred Stevie to howl joyfully in response to their exuberant energy.

After a fulfilling year living in St. Croix, my husband was presented with a thrilling job prospect in Seattle, Washington. The new role promised a fresh start and the allure of exploring a different part of the country, so we embraced the opportunity with open arms. The prospect of relocating signaled the beginning of a new chapter in our lives, and we were invigorated by the thought of the adventures that awaited us in the Pacific Northwest.

Stevie had consistently shown an impressive ability to adjust to new surroundings easily. His past responses to change reassured me that the transition to Washington would be another seamless adaptation for him. This confidence extended to our entire family unit; we anticipated that the move would be a straightforward and stress-free experience for us all.

Fueled by optimism and looking forward to the memories we would create in our new home, we began to prepare for the journey from the warm, tropical climate of St. Croix to the lush, evergreen environment of Seattle. I trusted that Stevie's previous adjustments were a testament to his ability to thrive in any setting, and with that belief, we set our sights on the adventure that lay ahead in Washington.

Just a few weeks prior to our planned relocation to Washington, our household grew by four tiny paws with the addition of a charming chihuahua mix puppy. His petite stature and whimsical appearance inspired us to name him Ratatouille, drawn from his resemblance to the rambunctious rodent from the beloved animated film.

Initially, Stevie seemed less than thrilled with Ratatouille's lively and boisterous temperament. Brimming with untamed energy, the exuberant puppy appeared to have an unwavering fascination with Stevie, following him at every turn, never missing a beat. Stevie accustomed to a more tranquil environment, needed some time to adjust to the relentless shadowing of his new, spirited sibling.

Despite the rocky beginning, the dynamics between Stevie and Ratatouille gradually transformed as the days unfolded. What started as a hesitant acquaintance bloomed into an unshakable friendship. The two dogs began to indulge in each other's company, with Ratatouille's youthful zest complementing Stevie's calm poise. Their interactions evolved into a well-balanced dance of lively play and serene companionship.

By the time we were ready to commence our journey to Washington, an amazing bond had taken root between them. Ratatouille and Stevie had become accustomed to one another and established a profound camaraderie, cementing their status as the best of friends. With their contrast in size, age, and energy, the unlikely duo now stood as an emblem of the affectionate and adaptable nature of pets, ready to support each other through the upcoming transition and beyond.

Chapter 12

Moving To Washington State

Upon our arrival in Washington State during the pleasant summer season, we were greeted with splendid weather, which made the transition all the more pleasant. As we searched for our permanent home, we temporarily settled into a charming garage apartment conveniently near the shore. The pristine proximity to the beach allowed for refreshing morning excursions with the dogs Stevie, Ratatouille, and Aki accompanied by the boys and me.

The Washington beaches, though distinctly different from the tropical paradises we were used to, had their own brand of allure. Lacking the warm, turquoise waters and gentle sandy shores lined with vibrant coral reefs, our new environment captivated us with its untamed beauty. The beaches here were a rugged tapestry of rocky outlines, sands adorned with enigmatic driftwood, and towering sea stacks that stood as guardians of the coast.

Amid this wild serenity, the dogs reveled in their freedom, eagerly chasing seabirds or playfully frolicking with each other. Meanwhile, the boys and I were enchanted by the whimsical tide pools, each a miniature world teeming with marine life a picturesque setting that encouraged exploration and fascination.

While this scenic wonderland offered new adventures, it presented unique challenges for Stevie. I learned to be particularly vigilant regarding two aspects of our beach visits. Firstly, the beach would shrink during high tide, water brushing up against large boulders that buttressed the train tracks above. On those days, I kept Stevie securely leashed to prevent any hazardous excursions that could result in him unassumingly colliding with the boulders.

The second concern was less predictable. At low tide, the beach would generously expand, exposing myriad smaller rocks scattered seemingly randomly across the sands. Some rocks were not large enough for Stevie to detect with his enhanced senses until he was too close to avoid them. Despite my attempts to slow him down or guide him away, there were occasions when he bumped into these hidden obstacles, sometimes resulting in minor injuries and a bit of bloodshed.

However, I would often reflect on Stevie's potential preferences. Given the choice between a restrained but safe experience on a leash and the freedom to roam with the occasional mishap, I sensed Stevie would always opt for the latter. The sheer joy he displayed at the beach was undeniable, a testament to his undiminished spirit and zest for life.

As the seasons changed and winter embraced the Washington shores, the low tides offered expansive stretches of beach. Undeterred by the colder elements, I maintained our ritual, taking Stevie to the seaside. His love for the beach remained unquenched, and no weather could dampen his eagerness to experience the sand beneath his paws and the scent of the ocean breeze.

When we settled in Washington State, we were acutely aware that we needed to prepare for the notoriously harsh winters a far cry from the perpetual summer climates we had known. Our wardrobe was notably lacking in winter essentials, consisting of only a few items suitable for the colder months.

In order to properly equip ourselves, I decided to take my sons shopping at Goodwill for more affordable winter clothing options. Stevie came along for support, as his comforting presence had become especially vital during the frequent migraines I had been experiencing since our move to Seattle. His service dog vest signaled his role and training, ensuring he remained calm, stayed close by, and refrained from pulling on his leash.

As we entered the store, the boys went straight to work, scavenging through racks of jackets, boots, and sweaters. Stevie was by my side, as always until a sudden and unusual distraction caught his attention. With a sharp turn of his head and an intense focus, he started sniffing the air, and his nose locked onto a scent so compelling that it triggered an instinctual response. Before I could react, the leash slipped from my grasp, and he was off, darting through the aisles after a trace of something significant.

Sean and Liam, noticing Stevie was no longer with me, began to frantically search for him. They were visibly confused and concerned as they asked why Stevie was not at my side and why I had let him go. Trying to downplay the urgency, I responded that the leash had slipped and that we needed to locate Stevie swiftly to avoid any trouble with store management.

Liam's quick thinking led him to scan beneath the hanging clothes by getting down to ground level, while Sean rushed to the front door to ensure Stevie wasn't heading out into traffic. Thankfully, Liam located Stevie by a sofa, set up as part of a display in the store's central area.

Rushing over, we discovered Stevie tunneling his nose under the sofa, his tail wagging with the excitement of a significant find. It was a first he had never before pulled away with such force. His behavior left little doubt that he had caught the scent he was trained to find: human remains. The implication was unsettling as we considered the history the sofa might harbor.

Curiosity piqued, my sons speculated lightheartedly about the potential scenarios linked to the sofa gruesome and innocent alike.

"Maybe someone had been killed, and the body was left there, causing blood to stain the sofa!" Sean suggested.

"Or perhaps an elderly person passed away on the couch, and their decomposing body was discovered days later, causing the fabric to absorb the decomposition," Liam added, smiling.

There was another idea that only boys would think of. I can't recall which boy came up with it, but they speculated that perhaps a girl had started her period while sitting on the sofa, leaving a menstrual blood stain behind. Boys will always have their wild imaginations!

I explained to the boys that even if such an event occurred, Stevie would not alert us about menstrual blood stains.

"But wasn't Stevie trained to detect blood?" one of the boys asked.

I gently corrected my sons' misconceptions about blood detection; I took the time to clarify the intricate differences between the scent of menstrual blood and that of regular, circulating human blood. I highlighted that menstrual blood is a complex substance and not solely composed of blood. It contains a specific blend of biological elements, such as endometrial tissue which lines a woman's uterus cervical mucus, and various vaginal secretions. Together, these components contribute to a unique scent profile distinct from that of typical blood, which largely consists of plasma, red blood cells, white blood cells, and platelets.

Throughout the process of Stevie's training to detect regular blood, it was critical to distinguish it from menstrual blood. To start, I ensured that his exposure to the target scent, which in this case was regular blood, was free from any other overlapping odors. Once Stevie became proficient in recognizing regular blood, I gradually introduced him to scent discrimination. This involved bringing in additional non-target odors, such as menstrual and animal blood.

During these exercises, Stevie's rewards were contingent on correctly identifying the regular blood while ignoring the non-target scents. This positive reinforcement was key in helping him discriminate between the scents, and through continued training and reinforcement, he achieved and retained high levels of proficiency. Thus, Stevie was trained to respond only to regular human blood, bypassing the presence of menstrual or animal blood.

When Liam, with a look of wonder on his face, asked me if Stevie was also capable of differentiating between human and animal blood, I affirmed his understanding. "Yes, Liam, human blood and animal blood each have their own distinct scent profiles. It's precisely because of the unique scent profiles that Stevie's training focused on his ability to discern and differentiate between the complex scents of various blood types," I explained. This training was what empowered Stevie to be so effective and precise in his work as a search-and-rescue dog.

As we attracted more attention from our laughter and the scene we were causing, I urged the boys to quiet down. The boys, however, playfully suggested that shoppers should be made aware of our dog's alarming discovery. They joked about a sign warning potential buyers of the sofa's morbid history, bantering about it humorously.

Recognizing the gravity of Stevie's reaction and its implications, I decided it was best to depart from the store. As we left, I praised Stevie for his diligent work, knowing his detection skills were as sharp as ever.

Once outside the store, Sean and Liam engaged in a peaceful yet animated discussion. They were puzzled how Stevie had come to identify the sofa as a source of human remains, given that he was adorned in his service vest, not his specialized harness usually worn for cadaver detection. As I walked alongside them, their voices, rife with wonder and confusion, blended with the hum of the streets, and I decided to wait until we were in the seclusion of our car to address their thoughts.

Settled in the car, I took the moment to clarify their curiosities. "The vest and the harness serve as indicators of Stevie's duties at any given time, like a uniform that cues him into what's expected," I started. "Yet those are just aids. Stevie's core service and detection dog responsibilities aren't dictated by what he wears. His instincts remain the same whether he has on his vest or harness."

"The fascinating element of Stevie's training," I continued, noting their rapt attention in the rearview mirror, "is his steadfast memory for the scents he's been taught to recognize like human cadaver odor. He's able to identify them anywhere, at any time be it when he's on duty or simply lounging around. If he encounters a trained scent, his 'super nose,' as you rightly called it, focuses on the find, and he knows to alert me, even if he's off the clock. His reward for this, as you know, is his favorite treat a fact he remembers well."

My sons' interest seemed to swell as they digested Stevie's instinctive response back in Goodwill. To provide them with a broader context, I delved into memory from our time in St. Croix that painted a vivid picture of what our dogs are capable of.

I shared that anecdote with them.

"It was a day much like any other on the island when I found myself in the company of Aki, my dutiful German shepherd expertly trained in narcotics detection. We were returning to our vehicle after participating in a series of medical training sessions I was undertaking to become a valued member of the St. Croix Rescue team. As we navigated the parking lot, Aki's demeanor abruptly shifted. Unmistakably attentive and singular in purpose, he stopped in his tracks next to a vehicle parked to our left. Without hesitation, Aki conducted a meticulous inspection of the car and swiftly alerted me to the presence of narcotics.

"The revelation was utterly unexpected after all, the idea of someone harboring drugs in their car at a rescue center's lot was, to say the least, surprising. Although I had my initial reservations, Aki's signals were unequivocal. His body language and the signal he made were clear indications of his detection, leaving little doubt about the presence of illicit substances within the mysterious vehicle.

"As I contemplated this unusual scenario, another student present at the scene, who had observed Aki's exacting behavior, approached me. She provided a startling yet plausible explanation: one of our instructors was also employed at the correctional facility and had, for reasons related to his work, taken possession of narcotics confiscated from inmates. He intended to transport these substances securely to the local police department.

"Hearing this, I was struck by the skill and precision of Aki's training, which allowed him to function with such remarkable accuracy even outside the parameters of a formal search. This unforeseen discovery reinforced the incredible training and instincts Aki possessed."

As I concluded the tale, the boys, caught up in the story's excitement, couldn't help but exclaim their admiration. "Mom, that's pretty cool! Our dogs are awesome!" they echoed in unison. Their pride in Aki's and Stevie's accomplishments was palpable, and it was a heartwarming reminder of the special bond and deep respect we shared for our four-legged partners.

From that day on, we made a family agreement: Stevie would be our first inspector for any pre-owned purchases. His approval would assure us that the items were clear of any unsettling past, securing peace of mind with his reliable sense of smell.

Following our memorable experience at Goodwill, I shepherded the boys to a different store, where we successfully procured the winter attire essential for the upcoming colder seasons. With our wardrobe now equipped for autumn and winter, we took the opportunity to familiarize ourselves with the area around our new home.

During our exploratory walk around the neighborhood, we were delighted to come across a pleasant surprise nestled among the verdant environment of the Pacific Northwest. Away from the hustle and bustle of the residential areas, we happened upon a set of captivating forest trails. These paths, seemingly undiscovered and untouched by frequent visitors, wove through the thick, rich woodland close to our home.

It felt as though we had stumbled into a secret garden, a quiet sanctuary where all of us, along with our dogs, could immerse ourselves in the tranquility of nature. The secluded trails offered a perfect retreat, prompting us to make plans to return and unwind amid the gentle rustle of leaves and the soft, earthy aroma of the forest floor.

Our beloved pets, with Stevie among them, instantly took to this natural playground. Each walk was an adventure; their excitement was barely contained as their paws hit the soft earthen paths. The persistent Seattle rain that some might find disheartening only added to their delight. The sound of gentle droplets on the canopy above accompanied the playful splash of their steps as they darted through puddles and mud, the cool air filling them with vigor.

What truly set these trails apart was their close proximity to the place we called home. It felt like a secret garden, just a brief five-minute walk from the warm quarters of our home. This meant that the raw beauty of the forest could be a regular part of our daily lives. Whether it was a spur-of-the-moment decision to take in the fresh air or a planned afternoon hike, stepping out of our door and onto the trails in the blink of an eye was a convenience that exponentially enriched our routine.

These excursions soon became a cherished part of our existence in this new place. The ease with which we could access the network of paths meant that the simple joy of being surrounded by nature was never far away. The proximity of this natural sanctuary offered us frequent respite from the busyness of life and a ready-made adventure for our energetic four-legged friends.

When Stevie first set paw on the trails, there was a palpable sense of caution with each step he took. Our previous life in the sun-drenched settings of Florida and St. Croix offered no parallels to the dense, emerald forests of the Pacific Northwest. The transformation in the landscape was evident, and the climate was in sharp contrast to our previous homes. But as Stevie became immersed in his new surroundings, there was a noticeable change in his demeanor.

Upon reaching the trails, his signature large, floppy ears sprang to life, standing alert as if each new sound brought a wave of excitement. He became attuned to the whispering chorus of the forest the crisp rustle of leaves stirred by the wind, the tranquil murmurs of a stream's flow threading through the woods. The atmosphere was alive with nature's symphony, and Stevie, with his sensitive hearing, was an eager audience.

Not just his ears but his nose, too, embarked on a journey of discovery. It twitched and quivered, sampling the rich tapestry of scents carried on the damp air. The loamy smell of the fertile ground, the intoxicating perfume of moisture clinging to the foliage it was as if every inhalation brought with it a new chapter of the forest's story. As he walked, the different textures spoke to him through the pads of his paws; the even softness of well-trodden dirt paths, the surprising crush of decayed leaves, and the unexpected textures of strewn pebbles and hidden twigs all added layers to his exploration.

Stevie's adventures reached new heights of excitement when he stumbled upon the gemlike hidden streams dotted along our path. Perhaps it was the distinct sound of flowing water that lured him, or maybe the unique, damp scent of streaming water intrigued his senses. Whatever it was, the enticement of the streams was irresistible to him, and he indulged fully in these serene encounters, standing with paws at the water's edge or playfully splashing about.

On one memorable expedition, an instance truly captured Stevie's remarkable adaptation to his environment. An unseen appeal at the peak of a hillock particularly enticed my dogs. Their snouts were deep in the underbrush, fervently investigating the aromatic clues. On my signal, they all propelled themselves into a joyous sprint back toward me. Stevie led the pack, his usual cautious demeanor replaced by a surge of spirited confidence. Despite his world being shrouded in darkness, his run exuded a clarity of vision a fearless dash that suggested a second sight.

"Stevie, if I didn't know any better, I'd think you could see perfectly!" I cheerfully marveled at his spontaneous burst of energy and sheer joy.

That moment crystallized a profound truth about Stevie. From then on, it became apparent that these trails had been transformed in Stevie's mind into a detailed map, every unique contour and feature ingrained in his memory. The manner in which Stevie seemed to visualize and navigate the complexity of his domain left me in wonder.

Upon welcoming Ratatouille, a petite Chihuahua mix, into our lives while living on the island, it became evident that he saw Stevie as a towering figure of comfort and protection. In the early days, the diminutive pup would shadow Stevie's every move, maintaining proximity to his larger canine companion. This vigilance was a sign of the little pup's need for reassurance, which he found in Stevie's steadfast presence.

Initially a tad resistant to this unexpected appendage, Stevie seemed to tolerate the persistent closeness with a gentle, if bemused, patience. However, as time wove its threads, an unspoken bond developed between them, transforming them into an inseparable pair.

Nonetheless, there remained instances when their fellowship paused most notably when Stevie was drawn into the spirited outdoor games with Aki, our German shepherd. Stevie would become consumed with a lively zest, romping and racing alongside Aki with unrestrained enthusiasm. In these moments of high-energy play, it was almost as though Stevie fed off Aki's inherent vivacity. His typical restraint faded away as he engaged in playful barks and chased eagerly after Aki, a symbol of their shared joy.

During quieter times, when the day's energy waned and gave way to rest, Ratatouille affectionately nicknamed "Rat" by those of us who doted on him found his preferred sanctuary nestled snugly between Stevie's hind legs. This was more than a simple preference for warmth; it was Rat's special retreat, a space where he felt most secure and content. Stevie transformed from a playful companion into a protective haven, provided a comforting fortress for his tiny friend.

In the sanctuary of our home, it became a familiar sight: where you would find one, the other was sure to be nearby. Whether basking in the sun, sharing a soft patch of grass, or strewn across the living room floor, Ratatouille was rarely more than a few heartbeats away from Stevie. Theirs was a companionship that defied words a harmonious, silent pact that spoke volumes of trust and camaraderie.

One peaceful afternoon, under the sun's warm embrace, I noticed Stevie resting peacefully outside. As usual, Ratatouille kept his faithful vigil beside him, a constant shadow to Stevie's presence. It was a scene that warmed the heart: the duo enjoying the gentle touch of sunlight. However, a small, peculiar action caught my eye; Ratatouille was attentively sniffing and delicately licking at Stevie's left eye. This unusual behavior from Ratatouille piqued my concern. Could there be an issue that had eluded my attention?

Drawing closer, I decided to examine Stevie's eye to ensure he was not afflicted with any hidden discomfort. Despite my careful inspection, everything seemed in order, with no redness or signs of irritation. Yet Ratatouille's persistent attention to Stevie's eye gave me pause.

"Is Ratatouille sensing something amiss with Stevie's eye?" I mused aloud, my worry rising. The possibility prompted immediate action. "It's best to be certain. I'll arrange for Stevie to see our trusted veterinarian, Terry, for a professional assessment."

Ever the inseparable companion, Ratatouille tagged along as Stevie and I visited the vet clinic. Dr. Terry was fond of Stevie, always greeting him with a buoyant, welcoming spirit. Terry knew Stevie's case was unique, as he was more than just a patient; Stevie had become one of the cherished members of his clinic's family.

Dr. Terry commenced with a thorough examination of Stevie's eyes. Each test passed without hinting at anything unusual until he measured the eye pressure. It was then that Terry's expression turned grave.

"Marina, I'm afraid the news isn't good. Stevie has developed glaucoma in his left eye. The pressure readings are alarmingly high; no doubt it's causing him significant discomfort," Terry articulated with a mix of professionalism and empathy.

My heart sank, a swirl of guilt and concern enveloping me. "I never realized he was in pain. Ratatouille was trying to alert us to Stevie's discomfort," I reflected, sorrow tinging my voice.

Given the severity of the eye pressure and factoring in Stevie's condition, Terry strongly suggested we consult with a specialized veterinary ophthalmologist. I immediately took to heart Terry's advice, securing an appointment with a specialist when we returned from the clinic.

After a fortnight passed, we faced the judgment of the animal ophthalmologist. The specialist recommended that the best course of action for relieving Stevie of his discomfort was to remove the afflicted eye a decision underscored by the fact that Stevie's sight had already been claimed by blindness. With gentle humor, they even quipped about Stevie adopting a pirate's visage post-surgery, helping to ease the weight of the decision.

As long as it meant alleviating Stevie's pain, I was resolute. "Let's arrange the surgery without delay," I consented, knowing it was for Stevie's benefit.

The surgery was performed deftly, and Stevie came through with the same spirited charm, unchanged by the loss of his eye. His enduring charisma and affectionate nature remained, proving that true beauty resonates beyond mere appearances.

With the arrival of winter, the first snowfall transformed our usual landscape into an enchanting realm draped in pristine white. The air was thick with excitement; my sons could barely contain themselves as they sprang out the door, followed by a spirited duo of dogs eager to delve into their very first snow experience. The sheer bliss emanating from the dogs was infectious, sparking a wave of cheer among us all.

Stevie, in particular, approached the newfound phenomenon with a momentary pause, his paws experiencing the unfamiliar chill and cushioned touch of the snow. This brief hesitation, however, was swiftly overcome by his innate curiosity. Soon, he was frolicking and bounding across the snowy terrain with wild abandon, his usual cautiousness cast aside by the thrill of this wondrous white world.

Our home was conveniently situated just a short distance from the boys' school, which presented a perfect expansive playground for snowy days. On this crisp and snowy morning, I thought it would be the ideal spot for us to embrace the winter atmosphere, so I gathered the boys and our dogs for a venture into the wintry outdoors.

As we headed to the school's open fields, blanketed in soft, fresh snow, the world was transformed muffled and serene under the weight of the white fluff. Stevie quickly dived into the day's fun, but not without maintaining proximity to his trusted friend Aki. For Stevie, Aki was more than a playmate; he was a beacon in any environment, a reliable presence that Stevie counted on.

As we stepped out into the gentle chaos of a snow day, Stevie continued his customary practice of staying close to Aki. Today, the snow had seemingly redefined the landscape not only sensory but audibly as well. Sounds were different, softer, and more subdued, yet for Stevie, Aki's steady panting remained a reliable and recognizable soundtrack amid the quieting effect of the snowy blanket. The rhythmic sound of Aki's breaths became a sound beacon for Stevie, who seemed to navigate the altered terrain with a remarkable sense of precision despite his lack of sight.

Stevie's ability to adapt was truly remarkable; drawing on the familiarity of Aki's panting, he could orient himself and follow his friend with confidence, almost as if the snowy ground beneath him was no different from the grassy yard they played on during warmer days. This instinctive reliance on auditory cues in a world that appeared so different to the touch and undoubtedly to the smell highlighted Stevie's extraordinary adaptability and the depth of his bond with Aki.

The call to end the day's snowy escapade was resisted, as the cold and damp had done little to quell my boys' high spirits. Eventually, coaxing my chilled sons and dogs indoors proved to be quite the task. Upon returning home, we noticed a collection of snowballs clinging tenaciously to Stevie's furry legs a side effect of his snowy adventure. These icy hitchhikers, though harmless, hindered his movements.

Indoors, we attended to Stevie with warmth and care, gently dissolving each frozen clump back into the water. Stevie's unceasing tail wagging throughout this meticulous process was a testament to his enduring trust and jovial spirit. Despite the minor inconvenience of his snowy attachments, his zestful energy remained untouched, a gentle reminder of the day's joyous moments.

I made the decision to become involved with a local search-and-rescue organization, bringing along Stevie and Aki, my two trained dogs. Upon joining, we entered the first volunteer group, which focused on cadaver training. The instructor and trainer there, Pamela, expressed doubts regarding Stevie's capability and safety in performing searches. Despite

Stevie's and my proven skills, consistently outperforming other K9 teams during training, Pamela refused to allow us to integrate into the human remains detection K9 unit, citing concerns for Stevie's safety.

Her reasoning didn't convince anyone; it was apparent that her reservations about Stevie's participation weren't genuine. Still, Pamela's decision was final, given her leadership role in the unit. There was no room for debate, and the organization excluding us did not consider my perspective.

Initially, I contemplated proving Pamela wrong by demonstrating that Stevie could excel in our certifications, showing that our team was on par or even superior to the rest. Unfortunately, Pamela's connections within the organization's upper echelons meant that her word was taken as law my efforts to challenge her decision were futile.

After reflecting on the value of my time and the lack of appreciation for my expertise in detection training, I made the decision to leave that organization. My aim was to find a search-and-rescue group that would recognize and value the contributions Stevie, Aki, and I could make.

After my transition to a new search-and-rescue organization, I discovered that my predecessor, Pamela, had harbored feelings of apprehensiveness regarding my arrival. It became apparent that my comprehensive background in detection training had made her feel insecure, and she feared that my expertise might overshadow her contributions.

The new team I joined, despite being located at a greater distance from my home, welcomed us with enthusiasm. The prospect of integrating a blind dog into their operations intrigued them, and they were eager to observe how he would adapt and perform in real-life search scenarios.

Understanding the unique training needs for a cadaver detection dog, the organization orchestrated a specialized session in an old cemetery. Prior to the session, they engaged in thorough discussions with the cemetery's administrators to guarantee that our training would not interfere with the sanctity of the resting places. The cemetery officials granted us access to a designated section suitable for our purposes, with the underlying condition that we conduct our exercises with the utmost reverence for the site and its eternal inhabitants.

This setting presented an unparalleled training environment, as undisturbed cemeteries like this one accumulate an array of decomposition scents over time. Such environments are invaluable for cadaver dogs; they provide authentic olfactory experiences that greatly contribute to their ability to detect and signal the presence of human remains. The diverse array of scents, each corresponding to different decomposition phases, serves to fine-tune the dogs' senses, enhancing their proficiency and reinforcing their investigative responses. The cemetery was not merely a historical site but a dynamic classroom for our cadaver dogs to develop and hone their critical detection skills.

We were preparing to conduct the search training in an area where a human body had been interred for no more than six months. The primary aim of this training exercise was to enable the canine teams to successfully identify and signal the presence of both recently and historically buried human remains.

The training was structured into two distinct groups to accommodate differing levels of expertise. The first group was intended for novice K9 teams already possessing some degree of experience, while the second was tailored to those K9 teams who were on the cusp of achieving their certification. Despite being an experienced team, Stevie and I chose to participate in the second group. Our lack of experience performing cemetery searches drove this decision.

The veteran canines were deployed first, and their adeptness within the cemetery environment became apparent. The dogs' excitement levels increased as their handlers led them closer to the targeted search area. Given that the locale was enclosed by fencing, it was deemed safe for the canines to conduct their searches off-leash.

The dogs initially engaged in a sweeping search by energetically running around the area. If this initial method fails to uncover any scents, they would shift to a more meticulous approach. This involved sniffing the air and systematically pacing between the rows of gravestones, resembling detectives combing through a crime scene. Watching these seasoned canines navigate the labyrinth of tombstones with such autonomy and precision was quite impressive.

As the dogs neared the source of the scent, there was an observable and pronounced alteration in their behavior this signified that they had detected the scent of human decomposition. Each dog had its unique way of communicating the precise origin of the odor to their handlers. These novice teams demonstrated remarkable skill, successfully identifying and pinpointing the locations where the scent of human remains was strongest.

As the less experienced dog teams were called up for their turn, it was our moment to step into action. Stevie and I positioned ourselves at the starting line, ready for our assignment. I diligently prepared him for the impending search, ensuring his harness was secure and all necessary equipment was in place. Stevie was always brimming with enthusiasm and eagerness, as was typical before any search operation we undertook.

The layout of the search area featured flat headstones, which posed no obstacle for an off-leash search. Planning to take full advantage of Stevie's abilities, I decided to conduct the search without a leash, confident that the terrain would cause no hindrance to his movement. However, the presence of a chain-link fence around the perimeter warranted a different approach before we fully commenced our search.

As we prepped for the task, another seemingly curious handler approached and questioned my method. "Hi, Marina, why are you not letting Stevie do the search off-leash immediately, given that a fence completely encloses the area?" the handler inquired.

I understood the confusion, so I took a moment to clarify. "I definitely will let him search without a leash, but he must walk around the perimeter fence first. Due to its chain-link nature, Stevie cannot sense it as he would with a solid barrier since the breeze can pass through it. For example, the fence doesn't register to him tactically as it would if it were wooden." I provided this explanation as I was making the final adjustments to Stevie's harness.

The handler nodded and posed another question. "How long does it take for him to grasp the boundaries of the search area?"

I smiled, proud of Stevie's quick adaptability. "Remarkably, it takes him just two rounds along the fence once in each direction and then he has a mental map etched in his mind. Also, Stevie is able to detect the textural change underfoot that occurs just before the fence, which aids in his spatial awareness."

With our strategy laid out and clear communication established, Stevie and I were ready to proceed with the search, a testament to the incredible capabilities of well-trained dogs and the importance of adjusting to their unique needs.

Upon completing our initial walk of the area for the second time, we reached a moment in our search when it was appropriate to unleash Stevie and entrust him with the task at hand. I always appreciate the opportunity to let Stevie conduct a free search; this freedom allows him to more effectively and thoroughly explore the environment. Once unrestrained, Stevie immediately bolted off, moving without a predefined route. His nose maintained a median position, neither hovering too high above the ground nor too closely skimming the surface.

It didn't take long for Stevie's searching instincts to become more deliberate, his snout now pressed against the ground, sniffing with marked intensity. This behavioral shift made it apparent that he had picked up a significant scent. He maneuvered through the landscape in a series of alternating zigzags and circular pathways, homing in on the precise location of the odor's point of origin. His search was meticulous yet time-consuming, but ultimately, his keen senses led him to a gravestone that exuded the most concentrated scent of human remains the site where a corpse had been interred some six months earlier.

Before reaching the gravestone, Stevie reverted to a low crawl, meticulously scouring the vicinity. The sound of his heavy, eager sniffs filled the air. Although he occasionally paused, his brief stops it did not signify he had definitively located the scent's source. Gradually, he crept toward a large tree situated in close proximity to the gravestone. Stevie inspected the tree's base, alternated his attention back to the gravestone, and then returned his focus to the tree one more time before conclusively signaling that the tree bore the strongest scent of cadaver odor.

The less experienced handlers on site were puzzled when I rewarded Stevie for his effective work, pointing out that he had not signaled directly at the source of the odor and also noting that he was the only canine to alert us to the tree none of the other, more seasoned dogs did so. I explained to them that the other detection dogs had been conducting their searches by tracing the lines of the gravestones. As these dogs have the benefit of sight, they integrate visual cues into their search technique in conjunction with their olfactory senses. I posited that had the gravestones not been present to guide them, the other dogs would likely have also signaled at the tree.

Furthermore, I clarified that Stevie did, in fact, display behavioral signs consistent with the identification of cadaver odor, actively seeking its source before determining that the most potent odor was concentrated on the tree. This phenomenon, where a tree's roots absorb the molecules emanating from a decomposing body buried nearby, is entirely plausible. The decay process is known to release various organic compounds into the surrounding soil, which the tree's roots can then assimilate along with other elements.

Highlighting Stevie's notable change in behavior as he encountered the scent was an essential factor it substantiated his indication of the tree as a significant point of interest relating to the cadaver scent, regardless of the final positioning of the odor source. This nuanced understanding of Stevie's behavior, along with the knowledge of how decomposition can impact the surrounding environment, is why I chose to reward him for his commendable performance.

During our time with the search-and-rescue group, we decided to take a more thorough approach to our training sessions. We started paying close attention to each dog and handler, observing their strategies for problem-solving during various scenarios. It was exciting to see how Stevie and I became the most frequently observed team. Witnessing Stevie adapt to his surroundings without relying on sight was genuinely remarkable. It demonstrated his exceptional problem-solving abilities.

One aspect that stood out was Stevie's remarkable sense of direction. He always knew the way back to our base or to the car. Over time, Stevie learned to follow my scent or track our path to return to our vehicle. It was incredible to watch him take the lead, guiding everyone confidently.

I vividly recall a training session when we were following Stevie's search pattern and inadvertently lost track of our own direction. After Stevie successfully found the training aid, it was time to regroup with the rest of the team. However, the three of us handlers found ourselves uncertain about the way back. We had been so focused on observing Stevie's work that we hadn't paid attention to our own orientation. I was feeling slightly concerned, as I had experienced similar situations before. Nonetheless, I had faith in Stevie's abilities, believing he would guide us back to the base.

I explained to the other handlers that whenever we were in the woods, whether it was for training or a simple hike, I would always say, "Let's go back home," as an indication to return to the starting point. Stevie quickly grasped the meaning behind those words. He didn't take long to associate "home" with retracing our steps.

And so, picture this three handlers, visually following a blind dog as he confidently led us back to the base. Upon our arrival, one of the more experienced handlers burst into laughter and remarked, "Isn't it amusing that the blind dog is the one leading the three of you back to the base? The blind dog knows where he's going, while the handlers seem a little lost!"

On a progressively dark autumn day, a sense of powerful silence enveloped us Stevie was surrendering to the isolating quiet of age. At eight years of age, a sobering reality had crept upon him; his once sharp hearing was diminishing. This deterioration struck a heavy blow to Stevie, a dog who had adeptly relied on his keen sense of hearing to compensate for his lack of sight to navigate the world with remarkable spirit.

Gradually, a noticeable change overshadowed Stevie's demeanor. Signs of disorientation and anxiety began to manifest as his world grew eerily quiet. Once guided by auditory cues, the comforting patterns of life now faded into silence. My valiant little explorer, known for his sparkle and boldness, became a shadow of his former self, shadowed by the disconcerting stillness. Clinging to my presence for assurance, he sought comfort in the tactile connectivity of our bond. Without my touch, he would meander aimlessly, giving up a palpable sense of helplessness in the once-familiar haven of our home and garden.

The sorrow of Stevie's difficult situation could not be overlooked. To see a creature of such fearless exuberance reduced to fearfulness was a vision of despair. The dog that once faced life head-on was now troubled by the unfamiliarity of his hushed existence, each day less certain than the last.

In my heart, woven with hope and sorrow, I sought guidance from Terry, our trusted veterinarian, a guardian, and a friend who knew Stevie's journey from the start. With apprehension, I communicated the extent of Stevie's distress. As Terry tenderly ran her hands over his frail frame, she held a gaze with me that softly braced me for the heartache to come. Her diagnosis compounded our fears: Stevie, alongside his fading hearing, was likely grappling with canine cognitive dysfunction, a cruel syndrome comparable to dementia in humans with confusion taking hold of his mind. Terry imparted her advice with gentle frankness, suggesting the time was near to consider the ultimate act of compassion for Stevie, to embrace the serenity of eternal rest over the turmoil that now clouded his days. She noted that Stevie was fortunate to have known the sanctuary of my guardianship, a sentiment that, even in its kindness, could not ease the profound weight of decision upon my shoulders.

A heavy feeling settled in my heart as I returned home like a weight was pulling it down. I couldn't ignore the fact that the time had come to say goodbye to Stevie, my dear companion. His constant state of fear and confusion had become unbearable to witness. It was clear that I had to make the excruciating decision to let him go, to release him from his suffering and allow him to find peace in the realm of dogs above.

After having heartfelt discussions with my family, we all came to the unanimous conclusion that it was Stevie's best course of action. And so, the day arrived sooner than expected when we would bid our final farewell.

It was late in the fall when I decided to make Stevie's last day with us extra special. I began by taking him and our other dogs on a long walk. To give him a sense of comfort, I paired him up with Aki, his trusted companion. Stevie always felt safer walking alongside Aki. The weather was perfect for our extended stroll, which I hoped would tire them out for the day.

Back home, my sons prepared our living room for Stevie's return, placing his beloved blanket and toys around to provide the familiar smells and objects that soothed him. After our walk, the whole family, including Aki and Ratatouille, our other dogs, gathered around Stevie. We sat on the floor, petting him softly, cuddling him, and speaking to him in gentle voices. We knew that Stevie, a blind and deaf dog, always found our touch comforting.

We then gave Stevie a treat he always loved a delicious roasted chicken. As he enjoyed his meal, a moment of happiness seemed to light him up, bringing back the Stevie we knew and loved, if just for a short time. His pleasure was clear as his tail wagged, and he ate. We all watched and savored this time of joy with him.

Dr. Terry, our veterinarian and friend, came to the house to make things easier for Stevie. When she arrived, she found Stevie lying peacefully on his favorite blanket. She had been there for us throughout Stevie's life, and today, she would help us say goodbye.

Terry began her work as we filled the room with kind words and love for Stevie. She started with a sedative to help Stevie relax and get into a peaceful sleep. As his body eased, I moved our other dogs to another room with treats to spare them from witnessing what came next.

After I gave a silent nod, Dr. Terry gave Stevie the final injection. It was a merciful act, ending his suffering as the solution worked quickly, allowing Stevie's heart to slow and eventually stop a peaceful and gentle end.

Dr. Terry confirmed that Stevie was gone. The room was full of sadness and the peace that came with knowing an end had come to pain and suffering.

Stevie's legacy endures, serving as a powerful beacon of inspiration through the memories we keep. He navigated life's hurdles with a relentless joy that never seemed to fade, no matter the obstacles he faced. His resilience reminds us to hold tight to the fleeting, beautiful moments that life grants us, finding splendor amid struggle and light within the dark.

His story is a touching testament to the strength of spirit a call to embrace life passionately and to extract happiness from the ordinary. Stevie's persistence to remain joyful despite losing sight encourages us to look beyond our limitations, adapt, and thrive.

Thinking about Stevie's happiness, I recall a day when Stevie was a shining example of happiness. His tail continuously wagged, an unmistakable sign of his everlasting joy. Even when he accidentally got a hollow bone stuck on his lower jaw, lodged behind the canines while chewing on it, Stevie remained calm and fearless. Rather than panicking, he proudly approached me, the bone still clinging to his jaw, wagging his tail with a sense of triumph.

Filled with concern, I exclaimed, "Stevie, my sweet boy, how did you get yourself into this situation?" But even as I spoke, Stevie continued wagging his tail, seemingly unaffected by the discomfort and potential pain. I called my son Liam, who was upstairs, and together, we tried to saw or file the bone off, but our efforts were in vain.

Realizing the seriousness of the situation, I suggested, "Liam, I think it's best if we take Stevie to the emergency clinic. They will have the necessary tools to safely remove the bone." And so, with Stevie wagging his tail happily throughout the journey, we made our way to the veterinarian.

Upon arrival, Stevie's tail wagged as if to assure us everything would be all right. The veterinarian technician was amazed by Stevie's unwavering happiness. Stevie emerged from the examination room in just a few minutes, free from the bone. Thanks to Stevie's cooperation, the veterinarian explained that breaking and removing the bone had been a simple task. To our surprise, the clinic delightedly informed us that they would not charge us for the procedure since it had been easy and Stevie had been so remarkably well-behaved.

In the end, Stevie's constant joy carried him through the ordeal unharmed. It gave us unexpected generosity from the veterinary clinic and served as a testament to his enduring happiness, even in the face of adversity.

In the grand tapestry of his memory, one can easily imagine him in an ethereal expanse. In this paradise, he is liberated from his physical constraints, running uninhibited through sprawling, lush fields. In that unbounded sanctuary, he leaps high, his tail a joyous pendulum marking each bound. With each playful spring and sprint across the heavenly meadows, he radiates the same happiness that defined his earthly journey.

The image of Stevie in this place of eternal bliss is a comforting salve to the soul, a mental picture that brings smiles even through the veil of sadness his departure has cast. It prompts a silent gratitude for the shared moments of love, the laughter, the companionship, and the unspoken understanding that echoed through every interaction with him.

Forever etched in the hearts of those who loved him, Stevie continues to be a symbol of finding delight in existence, encouraging all to seek out and relish the pleasure that life, in its ebb and flow, offers. His simple yet profound story is a timeless reminder of happiness's endurance and the grace in life's inevitable goodbyes.

Author's Bio

Marina Casanelles was born in Barcelona, Catalunya (Spain), and harbored a lifelong dream of training police dogs since her early years. The majority of her life has been spent in the United States alongside her family and beloved canine companions. Armed with two associate's degrees one in veterinary technology and the other in criminal justice Marina's academic pursuits reflect her multifaced interests.

At the core of Marina's passion lies a deep fascination with animal behavior, particularly in the realm of dogs. Specializing in dog behavior, she derives immense satisfaction from purposeful dog training. Leveraging her extensive knowledge and hands-on experience, Marina actively contributes to her local community by positively impacting the lives of both dogs and their owners.

Among the fortunate ranks of trainers, Marina's journey took an exceptional turn when she crossed paths with Stevie, an extraordinary blind dog. Through her interactions with Stevie, Marina gleaned a wealth of insights into novel facets of canine behavior. The profound impact of Stevie's presence on Marina's life ignited a realization Stevie's remarkable story deserved to be documented and shared.

Thus, inspired by the wonders she witnessed through Stevie, Marina embarked on a mission to give a voice to this exceptional dog's journey, fostering a narrative that serves as a testament to the enduring bond between humans and their four-legged companions.

www.ingramcontent.com/pod-product-compliance
Lightning Source LLC
LaVergne TN
LVHW020424070526
838199LV00003B/262